Image-breaking/
Image-building

Image-breaking/ Image-building

A Handbook for Creative Worship with Women of Christian Tradition

Linda Clark
Marian Ronan
Eleanor Walker

The Pilgrim Press
New York

Library of Congress Cataloging in Publication Data

Clark, Linda, 1937–
  Image-breaking/image-building.

  Bibliography: p. 142
  1. Public worship—Handbooks, manuals, etc.
2. Woman (Christian theology)—Handbooks, manuals, etc.
I. Ronan, Marian, 1947–   joint author. II. Walker,
Eleanor Myrtle, 1922–   joint author. III. Title.
BV25.C58   264   80-28896
ISBN 0-8298-0407-2 (pbk.)

Acknowledgments of the use of copyrighted materials are included in Notes,
beginning on page 132. Biblical quotations marked RSV are from the *Revised
Standard Version of the Bible*, copyright 1946, 1952 and © 1971 by the
Division of Christian Education, National Council of Churches, and are used
by permission. The quotation from *The New English Bible* (NEB) is © The
Delegates of the Oxford University Press and the Syndics of the Cambridge
University Press 1961, 1970. Reprinted by permission. The quotations
marked AB are from *Anchor Bible* (New York: Doubleday & Company, Inc.),
1965. The quotations marked KJV are from the *King James Version of the
Bible*.

The Pilgrim Press, 132 West 31 Street, New York, New York 10001

This book is dedicated
to
Eleanor Walker
1922–1979

| *Contents*

1.
Introduction

What Is This Book?

This is a handbook of ideas and resources for women who wish to take an active part in making Christian worship more expressive of women's reality. It grew out of a workshop that took place at Grailville in Loveland, Ohio, June 11–17, 1978. Long known for its creative work with women in education, the arts, and liturgy in the Catholic tradition, Grailville has in recent years sponsored workshops in feminism, socialism, and Christianity, and the "Seminary Quarter at Grailville" for women students in seminaries around the country.

"Image-breaking/Image-building" was designed as "an ecumenical seminar for women to explore the implications of feminism for styles and structures of Christian worship." The initial planners of the workshop, Linda Clark of Union Theological Seminary and Marian Ronan and Eleanor Walker of The Grail,° were joined that week by resource persons of various specializations: Renita Sheesley Banks (music), Sylvia Bryant (liturgical dance), Linda Robinson (body movement), Catherine Callaghan (linguistics), and Phyllis Trible (biblical exegesis). This core of leaders, some of whom remained the entire week while others came and went, functioned as resource people and facilitators for a group of about thirty-five other women who came to Grailville from all over the United States. The leadership nucleus

---

°The Grail is an international movement of Christian women with centers in Loveland, Ohio; Cornwall-on-Hudson, New York; and San Jose, California.

expanded throughout the week to include various participants who brought resources from their homes and parishes, convened special-interest groups, and facilitated small-group discussions. While the authors assume responsibility for the choice of materials included in this handbook, everyone who took part in the week has helped to shape the book.

We are particularly indebted to the Committee on Women and the Church of the United Presbyterian Church in the U.S.A., and to the Grail for financial support of this project. Thanks also are due Frances McLaughlin of the Grail and to Donna Dacus, Debra Branham, and Cindy Matyi of Bowling Green State University for their invaluable secretarial services.

Image-breaking

Anger and yearning generated the workshop: anger at the language, forms, and images that consistently ignore the realities of women's lives and experience; yearning to bring the universal dimension of women's experience into the prayer and celebration of the worshiping community.

We knew the dissatisfaction, confusion, and even rage we had experienced in trying to bring our whole selves into the existing forms and structures of communal worship. We knew that while many women shared our feelings they, like us, were isolated and largely unprepared to cope effectively with the monumental theological and sociological issues they sensed lay underneath their desire for change. How could any woman hope to take on 1,500 years of Christian history and the hierarchical structures of the present church over the question of naming the Trinity? How could one confront the overwhelming presence of sexism in the Bible? How could one change the worship patterns of millions of Christians, many of whom are insensitive to or even put off by the women's movement?

Underlying much of this confusion and anger is a healthy reaction against the use of exclusively male language to refer to God. From the most primary level of conceptualization—that of the creation of mental images—the idea that God is male controls our religious lives. Furthermore, we are surrounded by male-dominated structures of authority in the church which subtly (and not so subtly) subvert the reality that God transcends the gender differentiation of human beings. We live out male-determined views of our own sexuality as well as God's. Finally, we participate in rituals that too often equate openness to God's grace with submission to (male) authority.

As Rosemary Ruether has pointed out,[1] this association of maleness with God is a form of idolatry—idolatry of male experience. The exclusive use of male persons in the Trinitarian formula of address to God in worship reinforces this idolatry. As other women in the culture point out the relationship between language and the patriarchal nature of the social order, women in churches work to find other ways to name their experience of God, to release their imaginations from the stranglehold of the traditional male images, and to open up new and more universal ways of seeing and speaking of God.

Thus, we decided to bring together in one place women who were struggling to see and to say who they were in relation to God, to call on the power of our imaginations and our intellects, and to create out of our interchange alternative images of God and forms of worship that would be shaped by them.

Image-building

Since the purpose of the workshop was to generate alternative images of God and forms of worship, we knew that evoking the power of the imagination was central to our task. Throughout the week, sessions and exercises were designed to stimulate and stretch the use of the imagination. It is important to explain briefly what is meant by imagination in this context.

The imagination is a property of mind that, functioning below the level of the intellect, converts what are purely sense experiences into images.[2] Imagination is thought prior to the thinking of the intellect, the process that people usually associate with the totality of the activity of the mind. Out of the raw material of sensation and feeling, the mind creates mental images that provide the basis for the more abstract functioning of the intellect. These images are ideas of feelings and sensations. Most people are familiar with the mental pictures that pervade their thinking, but people also create "feeling pictures"—images of feelings. The feeling of cold is inchoate until the imagination creates an image of the feeling and we respond to it by saying, "I am cold."

To stimulate the imagination is to provide alternatives to the way people ordinarily envision themselves. Through the function of the imagination, the mind's eye searches beneath the often cliché-ridden notions of "who we are" to create new images from the uncharted, forgotten, or unacceptable aspects of our sense experience. These images provide new material for the intellect which brings it into relationship with the old, shaping new, more comprehensive perceptions of reality.

The imagination is a source of great power in our lives. In personal growth, many women are learning to tap their powers of imagination to release memories and feelings whose energies they can then integrate into the conscious direction of their lives. The imagination may at times put them in touch with the dark and fearful sides of life's experience, but it also allows the release of energies that are healing, enlightening, life-giving. The images that come to mind may be highly personal, idiosyncratic, significant only for revealing oneself to oneself. Or they may illuminate experience in such a way that they become a kind of revelation of the meaning of human life itself. Some of the most valued people in a community or society provide the others with images that become symbolic of common experience and give us new language for understanding and telling the common history. The Bible and all religious symbols, myths, and rituals have risen out of this work of the imagination. We must give this power much leeway to let it bring forth all its riches. Time and experience will tell what is of the moment and what may become part of the treasury of the future.

In the workshop our work with the imagination centered on creating new images of God. Thus our experiences of the holy became the object of the search—those experiences which are the foundation of our religious lives. However, all the work with the imagination, including that of creating new images of ourselves and of one another, could be interpreted as the creation of new images of God. If Genesis 1 is to be taken seriously, women and men both are created in the image of God. The image of God is female as well as male. By reestablishing the notion that women's experience can be a source of knowledge about God, we are righting the centuries-old wrong that associates woman with the malevolent powers of earth, darkness, and sexuality, and man with reason, light, and God. By refusing any longer to be carriers of the projection of evil, we are returning to the image of God the fullness of humanity.

Educational Presuppositions

The planners presumed a particular way of learning together as an essential ingredient of the workshop. Because of our educational presuppositions, we strove to provide a setting where women could examine, singly and together, the substance of their own religious lives—expressed in faith, theology, and worship—and find there resources for revitalizing their images of God and their practice of worship. The model for the educational practice was based on the following presuppositions:

1. It is a characteristic of our society that women have difficulty claiming their own authority. As an oppressed group, women have internalized their social devaluation to the extent that they consider what they do insignificant and trivial. They act this attitude out by giving their authority to others, particularly to men. Women can work against that devaluation by claiming themselves and their experience as authoritative.

2. In order to maintain the vitality necessary to carry the meaning of faith, religious symbols must be constantly transformed. This process of transformation is epitomized in the work that women are called to do to rid Christianity of the idolatry of the maleness of God. It is accomplished through the active reflection of communities and individuals on questions of faith and its expression in their lives.

3. The contradictions between feminism and Christianity are real, though not irreconcilable.

4. The imagination and those experiences which stimulate and express it, particularly the arts, are a powerful source of information and nourishment to the process of spiritual growth.

5

Thus the Week

After some initial input on the nature of worship and images of God, the participants in the workshop took part in a series of experiences designed to help them examine their own notions about God. That reflection formed the basis for the rest of the work of the week, which was more practical in nature. In an effort to emphasize the responsibility of each woman to formulate her own images of God, we attempted to modify hierarchical structures of education through self-directed learning, and we used resource people to stimulate discussion and facilitate interaction. In the discussions and experiments that grew out of the week's work, participants often differed sharply with the opinions and ideas of the resource people. (In chapter 5, in an article titled "The Process: Promises and Pitfalls," Meganne Root reflects in more depth on the educational process of the week and the problems we encountered as a group.) There was no effort to create a grand synthesis of the materials that emerged from the work of the group. Instead, we sought to help each woman see that renewed images of God lay in her own religious experience.

The process of reformulating the images of God took place within the context of a concern for worship. We chose this context because of the centrality of worship in the religious lives of most American Christians; many of the participants were in some way responsible for worship in the churches and groups from which they came. But our interest in worship was not only a practical one. Liturgical renewal is an expression of the deep need of many women to find collective expression for their changing insights into the nature of God and the human condition. These insights have grown out of their experience as women and provide a corrective to a tradition that has for centuries devalued and excluded them.

A mere description of the methodology of the workshop lacks the vitality of living through that week. It goes without saying that each participant would have a different version of the experience. The workshop had its high points and its low points, its critics and its enthusiasts. Its life took on the characteristics not only of the group but also of the weather and the place—

mid-June in the Ohio River Valley. It had a quality about it that we have begun to recognize when women work together anywhere: rambling, intimate, emotional, anxious, volatile, and very creative. The work women do together has an ephemeral quality that belies its power and tends to obscure the potential it possesses to transform our society.

Contents of the Handbook in Brief

This handbook consists of five chapters. This first chapter, Introduction, provides basic information necessary to understand and use the book. The second defines worship. The third, Exercises, contains descriptions of exercises designed to increase awareness of the participants' own religious depths, as a source of alternative images of God and the revitalization of worship. The fourth chapter is a collection of resources that emerged from these exercises, together with those brought to the workshop by participants, planners, and resource persons. The fifth chapter includes lectures and articles that were given during the workshop or submitted later as reflections on it. A bibliography follows Notes.

A compilation of the diverse efforts of many people, this handbook demonstrates the variety of approaches to issues that are important for women in our culture. In formal presentations and in rap groups, in scholarly exegesis and in silent movement, in argument and in meditation, we wrestled individually and collectively throughout the week with the many-faceted questions of feminism and the Christian tradition, women and worship.

How to Use This Book

This handbook has several uses. Most simply it can be a collection of resources for individual prayer and meditation or for enriching Christian worship. Further, it can serve as a guide to setting up workshops and retreats on the topic of women and worship. It contains a detailed explanation of the educational rationale for such workshops, as well as some theological reflection on the task. It provides descriptions of exercises that can be used, as well as enough information to transform those exercises for other situations or to create new ones.

The material within the handbook deals specifically with questions of sexism and the tradition and is an excellent resource for any congregation wishing to undertake the difficult task of changing the image of God in its liturgy. It can also be used as the basis for a project in liturgical renewal. The exercises can be adapted to many situations; they can enable women and men to experience and transform symbols and forms of worship from a number of different perspectives.

Finally, one is not bound by this book to work within the Christian tradition. It can be used to create rituals that express the depths of women's lives without reference to the vocabulary of traditional Christian symbols.

There is one final point to keep in mind about the use of this handbook, no matter who picks it up. One of its most important purposes is to stimulate the imaginations of people in a group to search out their own religious depths. To see it simply as a written record of the work done at Grailville in the summer of 1978 is to miss the point. *The book is a mirror and not a picture.* It is written to ask questions and to point toward ways of asking them, not to provide answers. Particular images of God, and particular worship forms and the theological assumptions on which these images stand, will arise from the answers of each group of users. Those answers recorded in the handbook itself are a set of responses that a once-in-a-lifetime, never-to-be-reconstituted group arrived at with joy and some pain. They belong to no one else. Their greatest value will lie in the stimulation they provide to pursue the search.

Why Use This Book?

Many of the answers to this question are implied in the preceding pages and particularly in the preceding section. The handbook is a step in the process of liturgical renewal that many Christian churches have been involved in since the mid-1930s. It provides material for the transformation of traditional religious symbols, a process that any tradition—not only the Christian tradition—must continually accomplish if it is not to wither away. It provides insight into the workings of the religious depths of a particular group of people.

For women—feminists and non-feminists alike—there are more important reasons for using it. They are both personal and political reasons, if one can differentiate between those two categories at all. We confront the issues this handbook addresses to overcome the impoverishment of women's lives (and men's lives too) that results from the idolatry of male experience in the Christian tradition. We work to offset the images of the woman as evil, as other, as property, as trivial, as invisible, as nonimage, by giving God our names and by naming Her ourselves. We search the scriptures for the God of Rachel, Leah, Rebekah, and Sarah. We create and use materials for prayer, meditation, and worship drawn from women's experiences of the holy to provide ways to enrich the Christian tradition within which many of us still stand. Finally, we pray and worship together to give ourselves the strength and wisdom to rid the biblical tradition of its sexism. It is a mammoth undertaking, certainly one women will not accomplish in their own lifetime or that of their daughters and sons. For this task, women need all the help they can get. This handbook can spread a little of that help around and evoke from women and the community to which they belong what they too have to give.

2.
A Working Definition of Worship

More than anything else that follows, this chapter is meant to be suggestive rather than prescriptive. Here we drop a few well-chosen seeds—a "working definition"—as a basis for further thought and for dialogue among women and men as to the meaning of Christian and non-Christian worship. The act of worship is above all based on relationships—to God and to the neighbor. As is true of all relationships, these are highly personal in nature. Each person must come to terms with the meaning of the act of worship herself.

Even the most cursory attempts to define worship show what a hornet's nest it can prove to be. We must first distinguish between the behavior or attitude of worshiping (the verb worship) and the event that takes place weekly in most religious institutions in this country. And focusing on this event in the life of Christians only makes us realize the more how difficult worship is to define or even to consider. Worship eludes the grasp. It is somewhat embarrassing when compared to most other activities in ordinary life. It has no tangible end product. It can be misconstrued as so much hocus-pocus. Yet we suppose it to be the central act in the life of a Christian community—one which has a transforming power even in its most mundane form.

For the purpose of bringing order to some of this chaos, it is important to choose a definition of worship and to use it as the basis for further elaboration. Take the one by James White which appears in his book *New Forms of Worship*. He states: "Christian worship is the deliberate act of seeking to approach reality at its deepest level by becoming aware of God in and through Jesus Christ and by responding to this awareness."[1] We self-consciously seek to approach the depths of existence in worship, and according to White we accomplish this in two ways: by becoming aware of God through knowledge of and experience of God's son and by responding to that knowledge and experience. There is a pole of awareness and a pole of response in this activity of searching out the depth of reality. Furthermore, White contends that we can get to the depth of reality through the person of Jesus Christ. This is a statement of faith; others may describe the process differently. Some Christians would emphasize the Holy Spirit instead of Jesus; some feminists would bracket out the reference to Jesus in the definition. In each instance, however, the event described is worship. All attempts to define worship end in theological discussions about the nature of God in whose name the community gathers.

One aspect of worship that is often neglected is the emergence of awareness from *response* to what we know. We learn not only by listening to the Word but also by responding to it. If we simply listen and do not respond, we have not succeeded in approaching the depth of reality. This emphasis undercuts our tendency to keep the worship of God confined to church on Sundays and expands the idea of worship to include those things that we are *moved to do* throughout the week.

In his definition, White neglects to refer specifically to the corporate nature of worship. The search for the depth of reality takes place among other people and is enhanced by that fact. "Where two or three are gathered in my name, there am I in the midst of them [Matt. 18:20, RSV]." There is a difference *in kind* between individual and corporate worship. It begins with questions of language and style and quickly moves into the nature of God. Theological discussion is essential, for it is out of such activity that a broadened understanding of God acting in our lives will come. This understanding in turn affects the language and style of worship we create; it points up the destructive nature of worship that is controlled by the idolatry of the maleness of God. Following Rosemary Ruether's lead, some of us may for a time have to bracket out reference to Jesus Christ in our own definitions of worship. There is no way to avoid confronting the contradictions between the almost exclusive use of Trinitarian ascriptions to God and the feminist analysis of the idolatry of the maleness of God in the Christian tradition.

But whatever point each of us has reached in that particular process, it goes without saying that many women want to take part in some form of collective expression of their changing consciousness about God. White's definition can stand, with some revision, as a basis for understanding and creating worship. The first step in that process is theological: the revitalization and replacement of symbols drawn from our religious traditions. From that point, we frame worship according to the nature of the community that gathers and the particular purposes of its meeting together.

We seek the God of Sarah as well as the God of Abraham, the God of Rebekah as well as the God of Isaac—the God, too, of our mothers, sisters, grandmothers, and aunts. The search itself is a form of worship. It is a response to the awareness that God's image is both male and female.

3.
Exercises: Image-breaking/Image-building

The following exercises perform the two functions named in the title of the workshop, "Image-breaking/Image-building." Through stimulation of the imagination, breathing exercises to promote responsiveness of mind and body, and simple experiments to bring coherence and structure to changing perceptions of women's religious consciousness, new images of God, new forms of worship, and new materials for expression are built. The act of creation at once breaks the hold that the old religious consciousness has over women and enriches and transforms the collective vocabulary of the experience of God.

The exercises themselves vary in format. Some are preceded by introductory explanations, some have very explicit texts, some are more suggestive than literal. Each needs to be adapted to the situation in which it is used. To repeat the appeal in the first chapter of this handbook, this book is a mirror and not a picture. In order for these exercises to perform a creative function and to stimulate reflection on one's own religious depths, they must be comprehensible to the people using them. Therefore, they must be cast in the working vocabulary of the particular group.

Provide plenty of time. Be sure that everyone understands the exercises, be sure the directions are clear. And remember, there

are no right or wrong answers. This is an opportunity for participants to recapture the ability to speak forth their own religious
reality—their own meaning.

Tapping Inner Imagery—Verbal Expression

The images of God imprinted on our minds and hearts have
come to us from innumerable sources—our parents, scripture,
the pictures in our first Bible, Sunday school, family prayers,
jokes, cultural expressions. But there are also sources from which
new images of God can emerge—images that we, as women,
can own and grow from. The kind of exegesis that Phyllis Trible
and other biblical scholars are doing, the history and anthropology of primitive religions, herstory groups, contemporary psy-
chotherapies—all can contribute to this needed refashioning.

During the past few years some of us have been developing
day and weekend programs called "centering retreats." In these
centering experiences participants work on relaxation (deep
breathing, body movement, visualization) and on very simple
sensory tasks (focusing on colors, smells, textures) as preparation
for coming into contact with their own images of God. Silence
is the context of all these activities. This workshop is based on
our experiences of centering. The hypothesis here is that when
women center themselves, using techniques that are not the goal
of the process but only its method, they will eventually come
into contact with their own authentic God-images. These images
are not God, of course, but authentic images point beyond themselves, and this is the ultimate goal of our workshop.

Participants gather in a quiet, comfortably furnished space;
pillows, mats, chairs, a sofa are all useful. The space should be
simple and uncluttered. A church or chapel may have difficult
or complicated past associations for some participants. Traditional religious images likewise sometimes serve to inhibit the
imaginal process. If participants have previously done sketches
or paintings of their images of God, these are ideal displays for

the workshop area. Other colorful objects, plants, calligraphy, or nonrepresentational art can contribute to the atmosphere.

The workshop leaders may choose to explain briefly the rationale behind the workshop, but this is not the place for an extensive theoretical discussion. Preliminary comments should be aimed at helping participants to quiet down and get in touch with themselves in preparation for the activities.

The following paragraphs are a suggested text for this exercise. Feel free to adapt any of it to particular circumstances. Leaders without much experience with relaxation and centering activities may tend to rush the participants through the various activities. As a general rule, going too fast is a greater danger than going too slowly.

"This workshop is designed to help you get in contact with your own images of God and to express those images and intuitions in words. We will be doing a number of relaxation exercises, sensory activities, and imaginative tasks that will assist you in the process of generating a series of God images that will be meaningful to you.

"You will need several pieces of paper and something to write with. The workshop will take about an hour and a half.

"It is important that you be physically comfortable, so find a pillow or chair that you like. Feel free to move if you need to.

"In order for most of us to do this kind of imaginative work, we need a certain amount of peace and quiet, so I am going to ask you not to talk during most of this workshop. There will be an opportunity for structured sharing from time to time, and, of course, if you need to take a breather, by all means take one.

"One last comment before we begin these activities. Some of the images we will be getting in contact with today emerge from the deepest, most intimate part of us and are not always easy to share. No one is required to share anything, but everyone is encouraged to express as much as is comfortable for her. I suggest that we all receive anything that is shared as if we were receiving a gift. Try not to judge your own images, or the images of others, as right or wrong, better or worse. Being judgmental will only make the imaginative process more difficult for you.

Let us also refrain from discussing the images and instead share them as we would a prayer."

I. Relaxation

"Please relax. Make yourself comfortable. Move around until you find the most comfortable position for you.

"Put aside any worries you may have brought with you. If it is helpful, literally stand up and go put your worries outside the door." *(Allow time for this, if necessary.)* "Anytime your concerns come back to you during this workshop, simply put them outside again. If they are worth worrying about, they will still be there in an hour and a half.

"Now I want you to imagine that you are expanding a tire around the middle of your body. Inhale very slowly, filling your diaphragm first, then your lungs. Don't move your shoulders. Breathe into your abdomen, and then your lungs. When you've taken in every bit of air you can, exhale very slowly, starting from your abdomen and counting slowly to yourself as you exhale.

"Now repeat this activity a number of times, inhaling slowly and counting while exhaling." *(The leader may prefer to go through the original directions several times, depending on the experience of the group.)*

"We will be returning to this deep breathing throughout the workshop to keep us centered and in touch with our bodies."

II. Vision

"Look around the room and notice the colors. Really take them in—give them a chance to speak to your eyes. Don't hurry." *(Allow at least 2 to 3 minutes.)* "Notice which colors attract you, and after a time choose one of those colors. Note the range of that color, how many shades of that color there are in this room." *(Allow 2 to 3 minutes.)*

"Close your eyes and breathe deeply, expanding the tire around your middle again and counting slowly as you exhale. Do this several times." *(Allow 2 to 3 minutes.)*

"Continue breathing. I want you to put your mind into neutral by drawing a large empty circle in the middle of your mind.

Choose one of the colors that attracted you and put that color into the middle of the circle in your head. Then fill the circle with all the associations that color has for you—memories, pictures, smells, feelings, people. Take your time. Don't rush. If you are patient, the images will come to you." *(Allow 5 minutes.)*

"Don't hurry, but be aware of when you have finished. Then open your eyes." *(Wait until everyone has opened her eyes before continuing.)*

"Close your eyes and begin with deep breathing once again." *(Pause for 1 minute.)*

"Put your mind into neutral again by placing an empty circle in the middle of it. Now put into the circle all the women who have been important in your life—in your personal history, as well as in human history—women in your family, saints, heroines, friends, teachers, lovers. Don't rush. As with the colors, give the images time to come to you. Continue your deep breathing at the same time." *(Wait at least 5 to 7 minutes.)*

"Without hurrying, open your eyes when you have finished." *(Wait until all the participants are looking up.)*

"Now I want you to write down the names of some or all of the women you put into the circle during this exercise. Along with their names, write something about each one of them— what they did or why they are important to you. When we have finished writing, we'll have an opportunity to share them with one another." *(Allow 5 to 10 minutes, according to the activity of the group.)*

"Let's take a few moments to share what we've written about the women we've been remembering today. When someone reads a remembrance, let's all respond, 'We remember you. We honor you.' Of course, everyone is welcome to share, but no one has to."

III. Hearing

"For this part of the workshop, let's stand up. Breathe slowly and deeply all through this activity. Stretch up, and try to push the roof off the building. Keep trying." *(Allow 1 minute.)*

"Continue standing until you need to sit down.

"I want you now to concentrate on your hearing. Listen very

carefully. Notice what sounds you can hear that are outside of this building [or this room, if more appropriate]." *(Allow 1 to 2 minutes.)*

"Now pay attention to the sounds inside this room. Try to notice every sound." *(Allow 1 to 2 minutes.)*

"Now put a finger in each ear and listen to the sound that is inside your head." *(Allow 1 to 2 minutes.)*

"Finally, I want you to listen very carefully for *a message that is being communicated to you.* This is a message from a source that only you can identify—some presence or power, nature, the cosmos, history. This message is especially for you and is within your own heart. Listen until you hear this message, then write it down."

IV. Responding to the Message

"Before we go on, I'd like you to roll your neck and head around on the top of your spine. First drop your head forward, and then bring it around to your right shoulder. Continue by rolling your head back behind you, and then over to the left, and finally back to where you started from." *(Demonstrate the neck roll.)* "Repeat this several times.

"For the next activity, I'd like everyone to close her eyes and keep them closed until I ask you to open them. This is to ensure privacy for all of us.

"Let's begin by doing some deep breathing, filling the diaphragm and lungs very slowly, and then exhaling." *(Allow 1 to 2 minutes.)*

"Remember the message you became aware of a little while ago. You may want to read it over. How does that message make you feel? Get into touch with whatever feelings that message inspires in you, whatever feelings the communicator of the message inspires in you." *(Allow 1 minute.)*

"When you are in touch with those feelings, intensify them. Really let yourself feel them. Then express those feelings in sounds, whatever sounds come to you, whether they are words or not. Repeat the sounds over and over, softly at first but gradually building up to as much sound as you want to make. Really express yourself. And remember—no one is looking at you." *(Pause until all sound has subsided.)*

18

V. Naming

"Before we start the next activity, I'd like you to sit in a comfortable position and relax your shoulders. We store a great deal of tension in our neck and shoulders, and that inhibits us. One good way to relax your shoulders is to use one shoulder at a time to write your name. Use your shoulder as if there were a pencil attached to it, and write your whole name. When you are done with one shoulder, start again with the other.

"Now continue with your deep breathing. Inhale slowly, diaphragm first. . . .

"This activity has to do with naming. As you know, naming is one of the great human powers. To name a thing means to have power over it. As women, we have had our names taken away, we have not passed our names on to our children, we have had God named for us by men. Today we will have a chance to write our own names for God.° The Muslims have an exercise in devotion that uses the Ninety-nine Names of God, and while we may not generate quite that many, we will have an opportunity to get in touch with some of the names for God that are within us.

"First, close your eyes. Breathe deeply and slowly. Now let yourself come into contact with what—or who—God is for you. Take into account the experiences of this day, other women, your history, your feelings. Let the images, the names for God, that are in your consciousness rise to the surface. When you are in touch with these images, write them down." *(Wait at least 10 minutes, until the activity slackens.)*

"Now let's break into groups of three or four to share the names for God we have generated."

VI. Prayer

"To begin the last activity, relax your neck and shoulders once again." *(Allow 1 minute.)*

"Continue your deep breathing. Sometimes it helps to imagine that you are a vacuum cleaner, sucking in a large quantity of air very powerfully, then exhaling it slowly.

°See pages 68-69.

"Now I am going to ask you to become aware of what it is you want—for yourself, for those close to you, for the world. Using the names of God that you have recorded, call upon God using one of the names and ask for what you want.

"You may have only one prayer—or you may find that you have many prayers. Whatever the number, when you feel you have prayed them fully, write them down. We will share these petitions with one another at the end of the writing period." *(Wait 8 to 10 minutes. Note when the writing has ended.)*

"As a final sharing, let's read our petitions aloud. After each person finishes, let's all join together in saying, 'So be it.'"

After this activity, have the participants write out their litanies, images, and prayers so they can be duplicated. Each person can then take home a copy, as a group anthology of the images of God. Some of the writing done during the original Grailville workshop may be found in chapter 5 of this handbook.

Tapping Inner Imagery—Visual Expression

The purpose of this exercise is to have the participants come up with their own visual image of God. The basic exercise has five steps:

1. Assemble an evocative array of materials—paints, crayons, paper of all colors, charcoals, clay, string, yarn, and whatever else may be available. Provide scissors, paste, and newspapers to work on.

2. Choose a passage from a poem, a story or the Bible—one which stimulates the imagination and is suggestive of God or how we may relate to God. Read it aloud once or twice.

3. Direct the participants to use the materials provided to create a visual image of God in response to the passage that was read. It is best to do this entire exercise in silence and with plenty of time.

4. Invite the group to share what they wish of the images they created, how they came up with them, how they feel about them.

5. Give the participants time to reflect on the entire exercise, either out loud or on paper.

The process of this exercise, however, is more complex than the five steps outlined above show. The atmosphere of the session should promote a feeling of trust among the participants, since the exercise is self-revelatory. Some explicit statement about gently eliminating the critic in each of us should preface the exercise, for example, "One simply lets what emerges on the paper emerge, without thought of posterity or the Museum of Modern Art!"

The materials chosen to stimulate the creation of the images of God should be simple, concrete, evocative—like the parables—not abstract or didactic. The directions for the project itself should be clear and grow concretely from the material chosen. For instance, you may choose to read the parable of the lost coin. You could then ask the group, "If you are the woman in the parable, what have you lost? Why are you searching for it so diligently? What does your search tell you about your image of God? In your notion of God, what do you believe might be the lost part of it?" or "What is the image of God that you search diligently for?"

Adequate time should be allowed for the completion of the projects and for sharing. When the projects have been completed, have the participants divide into groups and share observations and feelings about their images of God. The groups may be larger or smaller, depending on time, the number of people, and the participants' readiness to share. While many women may at first be hesitant to talk about their images, once the ice is broken they become more loquacious and the pictures in front of them become richer in meaning the more they work with them.

There is no obligation for participants to share aloud the thoughts they have about their images. However, there should be some sort of reflection on the experience itself—a period of silence or a chance to write down ideas in a journal. The creation of visual images of God is an important source of information about who we are and what we think and feel about the religious dimension of life and about God.

In the workshop at Grailville, this exercise followed Phyllis

Trible's lecture/discussion of alternative, female imagery for God in the Bible (see chapter 5, "The Gift of a Poem"). The session on visual imagery lasted about one-and-a-half hours, 45 minutes for the artwork and 45 minutes for the sharing of the images. Most people present participated, and many of the images produced were posted in the Oratory during the week.

Developing Awareness of Space and Its Uses

Sensibility to space is a faculty we often take for granted. Our instantaneous perceptions of space and the adjustments our bodies make to space go on without conscious thought. No matter how oblivious to what surrounds us we may be, we respond to space intuitively. We sense it in many ways—in depth, height, proximity, distance, as open or closed, oppressive or reassuring, in density, color, through vicarious touch, or smell. Light, color, sound, and smell all contribute to our perception of the space around us. Each of these physical reactions evokes an emotional response somewhere within us. The result is that a room appears either inviting or forbidding, and in it people feel comfortable and wait with anticipation, or anxious and want to escape.

The way we occupy a certain space also affects the way we feel in it. A group of people can huddle in a corner, avoiding the encounter with the space around them, or they can step boldly into the space, spreading out and claiming it for their own. Similarly, to change configurations within a space creates a dialogue with it. Space becomes articulate. Stance—movement—stance bring space to life.

The following set of exercises is designed to make a given space articulate. The participants will work with the space, creating alternative configurations. In each exercise, the participants will do something or say something to help experience space. How does it feel to pray standing in a circle? In lines facing one another? Throughout the exercises take note of what you feel. What attitudes are reinforced in each configuration? How is worship enhanced or diminished in each? How could you use space to help enhance the various components of worship?

For best results, use a space that can be completely cleared. Have objects that can be arranged and rearranged to reinforce various configurations. If possible, use a space whose proportions are beautiful. Since few churches have a large space that is both beautiful and flexible, remember that for these exercises flexibility is more important than beauty. Perhaps doing these exercises will promote the creation of worship spaces that are both.

The Exercises

1. Sit in pews or chairs arranged as pews with a center aisle. Say the Lord's Prayer. Stand and repeat the prayer. Now turn toward the aisle, facing the people across it. Say the prayer again. Mark the changes in your response to the prayer.

2. Clear the space. Take everything movable out of it. Move through the space, until you feel comfortable in it. Find a place in the space that you can claim as your own. Assume a comfortable posture—sitting, kneeling, standing—and say a silent prayer.

3. Gather into a circle. Repeat after a leader the following lines of Psalm 46 (RSV):

God is our refuge and strength,
    a very present help in trouble.
Therefore we will not fear though the earth should change
    though the mountains shake in the heart of the sea.

Next crowd in on one another, getting as close together as you can. Now again repeat the psalm after the leader.

4. Scatter to the walls. Stand there facing the wall and shout out the Lord's Prayer. Turn and do the same thing facing one another.

5. Gather in a circle and sit on the floor. Pick a topic of concern in your group or congregation. Have one person lead the group in spontaneous prayer on that topic.

6. Pause here for a time of reflection on the exercises, either out loud within the group at large or with pencil and paper to jot down personal reactions.

7. Choose one person from the group. Have her find an object to place on an altar or its equivalent. Form two lines through

which she and selected others walk as if in procession. When she returns to the lines, have everyone join her in order and make a procession around the room. Note how formalized movement changes one's attitude toward the space.

8. Move from the line of the procession to form a silent circle around the altar. Then move into a random configuration near the altar. Note how patterns change one's attitude toward space. Note how *changing* patterns changes one's attitude toward the space.

9. Select a leader and two helpers and have them tell the group how to arrange themselves. Then have the three take a space that elevates their status, vis-à-vis the group. Note how differing arrangements within one group affects the space.

Divide the participants into small groups to discuss the reactions to the exercises. Ask the groups to come up with some general conclusions about the effect of space on prayer. Note specific reactions to specific configurations as aids for the creation of worship space.

Working with the Language of Worship: Editing and Writing

In order to work effectively with the language of worship, people would do well to come to grips with the context within which they find themselves. As feminists we have been much concerned with sexist language, and rightly so. Yet this concern has sometimes obscured an equally serious problem: the overemphasis on language and reason which is characteristic of Western culture in general and of Christian worship in particular.

This emphasis on language can be traced at least as far back as the Reformation. The much-needed demystification of medieval Catholic practices led by the Reformers tended toward the reduction of worship to a purely intelligible experience. The Enlightenment reinforced this tendency. For many, Catholics as well as Protestants, worship has consisted primarily of reading, singing, and hearing words, with an organ prelude or some silence added, if we are lucky.

Before considering the practical problems of writing and editing for worship, then, we must come to grips with this prior problem. Any authentic critique of sexist worship must address the overly verbal, over-rationalized character of that worship, as well as the sexism of its language. As feminists we must continually emphasize that worship is a great deal more than language. It is the bodying forth of our relationship with that which is deepest and holiest in human life and beyond it. Any writing or editing for worship will be most effective if we remember that words are only one means of expressing that relationship. Words interact with ritual, silence, space, gesture, and music. They articulate feeling. They are never ends in themselves. They never stand alone.

Once we have situated ourselves within this cultural context and have taken into account the political and symbolic implications of our undertaking,[1] we can proceed to consider the individual text. In selecting and editing already existing worship materials, or in writing new material, it may be helpful to keep the following questions in mind:

—Does the selection further the purpose of the worship service?

—Is the selection authentic theologically? Does it express what the community believes?

—Is the selection pastoral? For whom is this service designed, and will their needs be at least partially met by this selection?

—Is the selection accessible? Will the members of the community be able to learn from their encounter with it?

—Is the selection strategic? What are my long-range goals in doing this work, and how will I be most likely to attain them? Will this selection help or hinder the attainment of these goals?

—Is the selection sufficiently beautiful to be used in worship? Specifically, was I (or the author) sparing in the use of words and attentive to questions of style?

—Is the selection sexist in its reading, its imagery, or its theology?

The question of long-range goals is particularly critical. Goals must influence choices in designing worship. For example, if a women's reflection group in a local congregation is invited at last to plan the service for Women's Sunday, that group will want to identify goals for that event. These goals may include arousing the congregation's awareness of feminism, or expressing anger and frustration at having been so long ignored, or broadening the image of God in that service as part of an ongoing educational process. The radical caucus of a national churchwomen's group will have different goals for a service they are planning. Whatever strategies each group adopts—that is, whatever theme, ritual, music, and language are chosen—it will be necessary to analyze whether they are aiding or hindering the attainment of the ultimate goals. Worship is too central and too important to be subject to anything less than careful planning and evaluation.

When considering this question of goals and strategies for worship, it may be helpful to think of two poles between which a range of strategy choices is available. One pole would be that of "nonsexist" worship. In some situations it will be most appropriate or realistic or loving to aim at reestablishing a balance between male and female images in our worship. One strategy could be to begin gradually adding a "she" to a "he," a "mother" to a "father," replacing one scripture reading with another, a meditation with a dance, until the images of God and of humanity begin to approach a balance, a wholeness.

The other pole would be the creation of a strictly feminist worship experience. Here the aim is to replace male images, symbols, words, and rituals with female ones. This strategy can result in the creation of an experience of antithesis, of dialectic, in a worship service, from which the experience of fully human language, imagery, and worship can emerge. In women's communities and organizations, in feminist educational experiments like the workshop at Grailville, and in other carefully chosen political situations, a totally feminist worship experience will be appropriate, and sometimes exhilarating. But those who wish to take part in such an experience should know also that it is guaranteed to produce strong feelings, both positive and negative, in the worshipers.[2]

Editing

When attempting to remove sexist language from written worship materials, we are confronted with at least three levels of difficulty.

On the most obvious level, the generic, we encounter expressions that refer to the human person and the human race as male. This situation can be rectified by replacing such expressions with broader terms like "humanity," "humankind," "person," "those," "the one," and so forth. But even on this level the task is not as easy as it might seem, because some of the substitute terminology can lack the concreteness and brevity of more offensive terms, for example, "man" as opposed to "the one." The exclusiveness of the English third-person singular pronoun (he/she/it) is also a problem. There is, however, a move at the present time toward using "they" in situations where "he" or "she" would have been used previously, for example, "When someone encounters such a situation they . . ." Although this usage can grate a bit on the ear at first, the arguments in its favor are persuasive.[3]

On another level, that of the image of God, our task becomes somewhat more difficult. In addition to the questions of goals, strategies, and contexts raised earlier, we also have to contend even more emphatically with the importance of the concrete in religious language. While God is neither male nor female, we have great difficulty imagining—much less praying to—a sexless, abstract God. As a rule of thumb, then, the concrete is always to be preferred—"mother and father" rather than "parents," and "sons and daughters" rather than "children." This practice can result in a lot of verbiage, however, and the *skilled* "editing" of biblical language or other great religious writings is no mean feat. Checking out revised versions by reading them aloud or sharing them with trusted and literate colleagues is strongly recommended. Be sure to acknowledge somewhere that the text is an adaptation.

On yet another level, some feminists object to violence and militarism in scripture readings and in hymns and prayers. There were, for example, a number of complaints about including Psalm 137 ("They shall seize and shall dash / my children on the rocks") in *The Grail Prayer Book*, but some of us are unable to edit out these images of struggle and strong feeling. We feel a need to symbolize the very real internal struggle and violence that most of us experience. If someone objects to violence or militarism in a particular passage, it would be more authentic for her to choose another selection altogether rather than undertake the difficult task of removing basic and often widespread images.

Certainly the most confounding problems we face in nonsexist editing come on the theological and historical level. As Phyllis Trible says, the patriarchal stamp of scripture is permanent,[4] as it is in many of our theological traditions.

In facing this reality, we women can only be true to our particular charisms. While some of us are developing a new hermeneutic with which to reinterpret our patriarchal history, others will be happier fashioning new worship forms that omit male symbolism altogether. The great challenge will be for women to understand the worth of both these approaches. We have little time to waste in renewing and refashioning the Christian tradition. It would be a pity to squander any of that time bickering over the validity of various approaches which may, collectively, enable us to achieve our ultimate goals.

Exercises: Image-breaking/Image-building

Although we are launching out into a new, feminist deep, we can set off only from the shore on which we stand. For a start, then, we recommend becoming familiar with some of the traditional written forms the church has used for worship.

1. The Greeting
May *(peace and joy)* be *(with us all)*.
Response: Amen.
    2. Prayer (or Collect)
You, *(O God)*,_____.
            What you have done, or do, or have promised
_____

What we want
(Forever and ever / Today and always / In the name of the
Set ending   *Goddess)*.

Response: Amen.
3. Confession

_____	*(We remember / We honor /*
Event or reality	*We acknowledge).*
	Response

4. Blessing

May _____.

Response: Amen / So be it / Hola!

Exercise 1: Choose either "For the Unknown Goddess" or "Veni Sancte Spiritus" or both (see chapter 4, Resources, pp. 69-70 and 71-72). Using the names of God and the petitions in these poems, write a greeting, a prayer, and a blessing. *(After 20 to 30 minutes, participants share what they have written by reading aloud.[5])*

Exercise 2: Select one of your favorite passages from the Bible. First, notice whether it is substantially sexist or only marginally so. If the language of the passage is only marginally sexist, make the needed changes and then practice reading the passage aloud.

If the passage is substantially sexist, that is, sexist to the point where you feel unable to use it, locate an alternative passage—one that makes the same point as the original selection or one similar to it. Then edit that passage for generically sexist language.

In both cases, make note of anything you feel unable to alter. Then share your passage by reading it aloud to the group. Comment on any difficulties you encountered during the process of choosing and editing.

Exercise 3: (A collection of hymnals from the major Christian denominations should be made available for this exercise.)
Many women have ceased to enjoy some once-favorite hymns because of their wording. Choose one or more of these hymns and try to edit out the sexist language without ruining the hymn. Feel free to drop the most difficult stanza.

When you have finished, sing the hymn aloud, either to the

group or off in a corner alone if you prefer. Singing newly edited hymns aloud is the acid test.

Exercise 4: While careful editing well in advance of a liturgy or service is the ideal, most of us sooner or later are asked to stand up with very little preparation and read a scripture passage aloud. This is the moment that separates the editors from the also-rans. The only thing to do in this kind of situation is plunge in.

Choose a partner. Each select a passage from the Bible and assign it to the other to read.

Skim through the selection for two or three minutes, then read it aloud, attempting to remove as much offensive language as possible. Make note of the difficulties you encounter and check them out with your partner. When one of you is finished, the other follows suit.

Copyrights

A word of caution must be said about both using and "editing" copyrighted material. Although "fair use" is not defined in word count and some copyright owners permit the use of as many as five hundred words without permission, any material that is a complete work—such as a prayer and a litany—requires permission regardless of length. Poetry and hymns (both words and tunes) in copyright always require permission for reprinting.

While a worship leader or participant may use and even "edit" copyrighted material orally, such material may not be copied or reproduced for distribution, as in a worship program, without permission. Common decency requires that even oral editing be acknowledged as adaptation or paraphrase. When asking for permission to reprint copyrighted material, be sure to indicate what changes you want to make.

Publishers may not own copyrights on some creative works, but they usually handle permissions for authors and composers. For additional information on copyrights, refer to such denominational publications as *Inclusive Language Guidelines for Use and Study in the United Church of Christ* (June 1980) or write to Register of Copyrights, Library of Congress, Washington, D.C. 20559. *A Musician's Guide to Church Music* by Joy E.

Lawrence and John A. Ferguson (New York: The Pilgrim Press, 1981) has excellent information on copyrights in Appendix A.

Freeing the Voice for Worship

The rationale behind a voice workshop is that the singing voice is a primary vehicle for religious experience, both in corporate worship and in private meditation. The voice, if properly attended to, can be the means of approaching and experiencing the Holy or Other. Unfortunately, the voice is often overburdened by unnecessary expectations as to how it "should" sound and how it should be used, both in worship and in singing for the fun of it. Too often self-images and images of how people should praise God restrict rather than enhance expression and experience.

A voice workshop of this nature needs a leader who has had some experience with the kind of techniques described below. Such techniques are not necessarily part of the vocabulary of the singer or the singing teacher, however accomplished they may be. They are instead more like a "zen of singing"—forgetting conscious achievement and letting the natural functioning of breathing and vocal cords take over.

Such a voice workshop seeks to give participants the opportunity to attend to their voices as unique and as rooted deeply in their bodies. Each session begins with physical exercises in relaxation and breathing that aim at releasing energy that often gets caught in the throat and inhibits free vocal expression. Each singer is encouraged to listen nonjudgmentally to her voice and to let it tell her about herself. This means avoiding such labels as "soprano/alto" and "strong/weak."

Any number of songs, exercises, and vocal games can be used as the basis for this work. For example, lying on the floor, breathing naturally, and humming or singing a range of different notes allows participants to experience a more natural voice placement and a wider range than they are used to. Sitting on a chair and hanging the head loosely between the legs while singing helps to reduce tension in the shoulders and in the throat muscles so that participants experience what relaxed singing feels like.

When participants have begun to experience their voices

more freely, they can start experimenting with different ways the voice has been and can be used in worship. Chanting—reciting words in the natural rhythm of speech on slow, even exhalation of the breath—is a powerful asset to meditation. A chant of the Magnificat, done antiphonally (two groups alternating verses), demonstrates a very old practice of singing. On-the-spot improvisation of a psalm can be used; have the participants try to let their voices be totally informed by the rhythms and inflections of the text. "Lining out" an early American hymn—a process in which a leader sings a line or two and the group repeats it, sometimes with variation—demonstrates still another usage and helps to free the voice both rhythmically and melodically. Finally, singing rounds combines and develops those forms that have come before. An enthusiastic round is an apt example of the feminist perspective. A round invites participation from everyone; it is a group experience rather than solo or chosen choir; it is a blending and an acceptance of difference.

Guiding Meditation

Silence is a profound inducement to prayer. Long silences give us enough time to settle down, slow down, and find a center of quiet amid the whirling, buzzing life of the mind.

Gather in a room free of clutter. Find a comfortable position. Do simple breathing exercises to aid the centering process.

Here is a suggested format for a meditation. It can be adapted to particular circumstances.

"Take a few slow deep breaths. Watch the breath coming in and out of your body. Now begin counting your breaths. Count up to four and then begin again at one. When your mind begins to wander, say to yourself, 'My mind is wandering,' and then begin counting again."

A leader reads a poem or a passage of scripture, waits, and then repeats it or a few striking images in it. The reading forms the silence. Each woman may use the silence as she wishes: picking up phrases and repeating them to herself, noting emotions evoked by the text, reflecting on events in her life in terms of the text, or simply resting. The selection is then read a third time. Silence ends the session.

Silence is rarely used in worship services. When it occurs it sets people off-balance; they think someone has forgotten to do something! However, it is an effective form of worship. It acts as a punctuation mark between parts of worship. It serves to focus the parts and make them more significant. It gives the worshiper time to become aware of what is happening in the deep recesses of the soul and to assimilate ideas and feelings evoked by worship.

Suggestions for texts to be used in guided meditation include "For the Unknown Goddess" by Elizabeth Brewster (pages 69-70, below), "Meditation on Luke 1" by Dorothee Soelle (pages 73-74, below), and "Crossing a Creek" and "Thaw" by Martha Courtot (pages 75-76 and 54, below), as well as the story of the woman with the ointment (Luke 7:36-50) or other biblical texts.

Working with Ritual

Ritual is an integral part of life, common to all cultures. It provides forms through which people meet, carry out social activities, celebrate, commemorate. The forms of any given ritual may be understood by only a few initiates or by most of the population. The acts performed may be relatively casual or deeply meaningful. They may be secular or sacred, although the most enduring rituals usually have some present or previous connection with the sacred.

At its most minimal level, ritual can be described as "an agreed upon pattern of movement."[6] This statement says nothing about the meaning a ritual may have. Examples of the kinds of ritual that permeate everyday life are the ways we greet one another, such as a handshake, or the ways we assist one another going in and out, crossing the street, getting in or out of cars. There are whole sets of rituals for events like the ballgame, with its customary foods, cheering, codes of behavior for players and spectators, or the symphony concert, with its formal dress and protocol for concert master, conductor, and soloist in appearing, receiving applause, and so on.

Defining ritual as "a corporate symbolic action" would point more to the kinds and levels of meaning the word may embody and would be true of rituals connected with worship. Each of the words in this definition is important:

Ritual is an *action*. People gather in a certain place, in a certain manner, for a certain purpose; they walk, sit, stand, speak, gesture, use objects, wear dress significant to the action, and so on.

Ritual is *corporate*. It is performed by people together. Even if one person alone may perform part of the action, its meaning is dependent on the corporate understanding of the whole action.

Ritual is *symbolic*. The action has a meaning which it exemplifies and embodies, at least in schematic form, and which is made present in and through the action to those who participate in it. The ritualized action may commemorate a past event of great significance to the community (as Passover commemorates the escape of the Hebrew people from slavery to freedom) or express the social significance of acts performed by individuals, such as taking a spouse and thus becoming a potential child-bearer. The daily action of eating is ritualized in many different ways, according to the occasion (picnic, banquet, or act of worship) and to the kind of significance invested in it.

One characteristic of ritual that is inherent in its corporate, symbolic function is its use of the power of repetition. Repetition is not of itself dead or deadening. It is deadening only when the meaning is trivial or has ceased to be relevant to the community's life. Repetition may in fact serve to maintain rituals even when their meaning has been obscured or changed. (Mardi Gras, which no longer precedes any real lenten fast, and most of the traditions associated with Christmas—tree, yule log, holly, gift-giving, which have lost their original, pre-Christian connections with winter solstice, renewal of the earth, sexuality—are prime examples.) If no new meaning is given the ritual, it will of course eventually disappear. But there are many examples of rituals that have survived a period of formalism and trivialization and then regained a new if altered life by being invested with renewed meaning from the experience and worldview of the people using them.

Problems and Guidelines

If we are going to work with the renewal or creation of ritual in worship, we need to recognize some of the questions we will have to deal with as we adapt or design rituals for use in particular situations.

Our greatest problem with ritual is the loss, diffusion, or fragmentation of the meanings that our symbols and rituals, particularly our religious rituals, are undergoing at the present time. There are many reasons for the malaise women feel with certain biblical, liturgical, and theological images and ways of thinking, and much has been written about these changes. We shall limit ourselves to what seems to have most bearing on our attempts to renew the forms and language of worship from women's experience.

We have lost contact with the kind of culture in which much of our inherited symbol system was developed, a culture in which agriculture was primary and in which alliance with the forces and cycles of nature was vitally important for human survival. A new awareness of the way patriarchy has molded the biblical origins and the church's interpretation of Christianity has both sharpened and refocused this observation. Present-day ecological concerns are in some sense a renewal of the awareness of the earth and the profound linkages of life processes with the forces of the cosmos. Some feminist pursuits of a spirituality drawing on our bonds with the vital forces of earth are at least in part a search for alternatives to the patriarchal (or "sky") aspects of religion, since it is unlikely that twentieth-century women will embrace former fertility cults or that the twentieth or twenty-first centuries will return to the kind of intimacy with nature that was an absolute necessity for the survival of pre-industrial cultures.

Some have suggested that the loss of contact with nature has led not only to the withering of meaning of particular symbols, but also to near atrophy of our symbolic thinking. But our need and capacity for image-making has not been altered. If our culture does not provide us with the former rich context for developing and expressing images, we are finding other, perhaps more self-conscious means of access to their creative power.

Assuming that we have the ability to create symbols, women

are still faced with questions and uncertainties about the value and meaning of many traditional symbols and rituals. We are no longer sure what certain rites or symbols, even those of our own tradition, mean to ourselves or to others. Even if women continue to find meaning for themselves personally in traditional forms, the corporate meaning essential to ritual can no longer be counted on. The disaffection women may feel with institutional authority, particularly when it is used to exclude us or others from full access to worship or ministry, is no doubt one factor that weakens the corporate fabric of worship.

The complexity of the situation with regard to ritual makes the role of the creative imagination more central than ever. We must unlock our own inner riches. We must learn to listen also to poets and musicians, to the many kinds of artists who can express the feeling and vision of the times. We must approach the work of designing, renewing, or adapting rituals with great sensitivity to the meanings they bear and to the meanings we wish to give them.

In conclusion, we would like to use words of Margaret Mead:

A good ritual . . . like a natural language . . . has been spoken for a very long time by very many kinds of people. . . . It must be old, otherwise it is not polished. It must be old, otherwise it cannot reflect the play of many imaginations. It must be old, otherwise it will not be fully available to everyone born within that tradition. Yet it also must be alive and fresh, open to new vision and changed vision.

The essence of ritual is the ability of the known form to reinvoke past emotion. . . .

Celebrations answer the needs of each age: of the youngest child, first enthralled by the lights of candles on a cake; . . . of great-grandparents, living longer than people have ever lived and trying hard to learn how to remain in touch with the modern world. A celebration must be a ceremony in which each finds something of his/her own and all share something together. It must be a community ceremonial if it is to have a place for each of them. . . . If we are to have real celebrations that do not pall or peter out because of the shallowness of their inspiration, we must have an informed and exciting mix of the ceremonial inventions of other ages and other people. Only thus can the new sparkle like a jewel in a setting which, because it is familiar, sets it off.[7]

Creating Ritual: Exercises
To work out the exercises that follow, or any other ritual, think about and then apply the following guidelines:

Three general criteria:
1. The best rituals are the most economical in their use of words and gestures in relation to the meaning they are intended to express.
2. The best rituals make it possible for the whole community to take part in them with authenticity.
3. The meaning of the ritual is to be expressed as fully and directly as possible by the words and the actions used, so that additional explanation is not necessary.

Some steps to take:
1. Get in touch with the deepest, most authentic meaning of the event for the celebrating community.
2. Get in touch with feelings you or others may have about the event, so that they can be recognized and taken account of in designing the action.
3. Find what bodily attitudes, gestures, or movements arise from and express the meaning, with its attendant feelings.
4. Decide how these attitudes, gestures, or movements can be expressed corporately.
5. If any traditional symbolic actions or gestures are used, be sure their meaning is available and authentic to the community.
6. Decide what words will reinforce the meaning of the action.
7. Determine what context of space, surroundings, readings, music, etc., will enrich and enhance the action.

Exercises in Ritual-planning

   a. Welcoming a new baby into your community
   b. Moving into a new house or apartment
   c. Expressing support for a group engaged in a difficult action, e.g., the coal miners on strike
   d. Reconciliation between two groups or factions that have been in conflict
   e. Support for a person who is seriously ill
   f. Celebrating the reaching of puberty for a young woman
   g. Celebrating a woman's fiftieth birthday
   h. Recognizing the end of a close relationship
   i. Sharing money or other material resources of a group for a recognized need
   j. Planting a garden
   k. Celebrating the harvest of the fruits of a garden

These exercises do not include examples of events or occasions for which a major Christian ritual tradition already exists, such as baptism, marriage, or burial, but are instead chosen to stimulate reflections on events which may be important in our lives but for which ritual forms are not readily available.

Our work with traditional rituals may have as its focus one or more goals, for example, to deepen our understanding of their meaning so as to make it more obvious, to tie them more closely to our contemporary experience so that both the experience and the tradition may be illuminated, or to expand the meaning to include new experience and make it more meaningful to the participants.°

°Several examples of the rituals developed at "Image-breaking/Image-building" may be found in chapter 4, Resources, pages 48-60.

4.
Resources

This chapter includes worship services, antiphons, rituals, prayers, and poems that were developed at the "Image-breaking/Image-building" workshop or were brought to that workshop by participants. In some cases, related resources have been added to the collection.

The selections were written by individuals of different ages, denominations, and celebratory styles from different sections of the country. These resources can be useful in designing your own unique forms of worship. At best they may be suggestive of the creative possibilities available to you and to the groups of which you are part.

Worship Services

Opening Prayers: "Image-breaking/Image-building" Workshop

ENTRANCE
"I Wish I Knew How It Would Feel to Be Free"—Nina Simone (*recorded*)

INVOCATION[1]
Leader: In the name of God, the mother and father of all life, in the name of the Son, who liberates us, and in the name of the Spirit, who keeps us going with love and power.

All: We celebrate your presence as we worship together. We also celebrate our presence because we are glad to be here to share our humanness and our faith. It's great to be alive!

READINGS
I. Genesis 3:1-7
II. The Mountain-moving Day°—Yosano Akiko
III. From *Between Myth and Morning*†—Elizabeth Janeway

SONG
"I Wish I Knew How It Would Feel to Be Free" *(all)*

LITANY OF THANKSGIVING[2]
Leader: We commemorate women in the Bible who were strong leaders and servants:

Old Testament women who demonstrated their faith in Yahweh;

New Testament women who showed their love for Christ;

Esther, who risked her life so that her people could live;

Mary Magdalene, who was the first witness to Christ's resurrection.

All: Help us to follow their example of faith and love.
Leader: We also remember women in the past who lived what they believed in:

Sojourner Truth, a former slave who became an abolitionist and feminist orator;

Harriet Tubman, a black slave woman who gained her freedom and then organized the underground railroad that brought three hundred women, men, and children out of bondage;

Elizabeth Cady Stanton and Susan B. Anthony, who for fifty years planned, organized, and strategized

°See pages 76-77.
†Elizabeth Janeway, *Between Myth and Morning: Women Awakening* (New York: William Morrow & Co., 1974). Select a passage suited to the needs and interests of your group.

for the women's movement until it became a national force.

All: They struggled for freedom. Help us to struggle, God, and to learn and grow as we struggle, not only for our own personal freedom, but for freedom for all people.

Leader: We also remember the women of our own time who have not forgotten how to smile, laugh, dance, sing, and celebrate:
who continue to struggle,
who have meaningful lives,
who help sisterhood bloom,
who listen and cry and drink coffee together.

All: We praise you, God, for the strength and courage of all our sisters.

Leader: Let us also remember special women in our lives:

(Here the participants share their remembrances; after each the group responds:)

All: We praise you, O God, for this woman.

LIBERATION OF THE APPLES

As we share in the eating of these apples
We reject Man's traditional interpretation of the Adam and
    Eve story.
We affirm that the story does not convey truth to us about
    ourselves.
We hold that Eve performed the first free act.
We pledge ourselves to communicate and to collaborate in
    developing the human tradition, the whole truth, for the
    liberation of women and men and the whole of creation.

HYMN°

Lauds

Lauds, or Morning Prayer, is one of the seven traditional "hours" of common prayer which for centuries marked the rhythm of

---

°Close with a hymn on the theme of freedom that is familiar to your group.

the monastic day and in revised form is still in use today. During the workshop we chose to open each day with an adapted form of Lauds as an example of the timeless value of certain traditional structures for worship. The elements of Lauds are as follows:

Opening
A short versicle and response, taken from the psalms and usually followed by a doxology. The versicle in its various forms asks God to assist in the offering of the prayer. This opening helps participants to enter into the presence of God and to renew their awareness of the act of prayer they are undertaking.

Hymn
Any good hymn, ancient or modern, from Christian hymnody may be used. For morning prayer, hymns of praise or thanksgiving for the day, for creation, or for new life are appropriate.

Psalms
The psalms of Lauds are generally psalms of praise suited to the beginning of a new day. In the days when all the hours of the traditional office were recited the entire psalter was covered each week. In the revised version, it is covered once every four weeks. The familiarity that ensued from constant repetition made the psalms highly suitable for meditation. The practice of chanting enhanced that meditative quality, since it coordinated recitation with breathing. Using the rhythm of breathing as a basis for meditative prayer is a practice common to many religious traditions. Keeping the flow of breath even, avoiding emphasis or expression of feeling, and listening to others so that all seem to be praying with one voice do much to deepen the meditative character of the recitation.

The group praying together is divided into two "choirs" that recite one verse at a time in alternation. A slight pause is made in the middle of each verse. The effect of the alternation is that one side recites a verse on a long, slow exhalation, then rests while the other side picks up the breath, so that one verse flows evenly into the next. A cantor usually intones whatever parts are to be sung, reads the single voice lines of versicle and responsory, and introduces the recitation of each psalm by reading the first verse up to the pause in the middle, where it is picked up by the whole first choir. It may take a group some time to master the coordination of breath and recitation, but when the flow and the unity are achieved the recitation is far more satisfying than the usual haphazard collective reading.

The content of the psalms also needs to be sufficiently assimilated to become matter for meditation. It may well take some wrestling with the contents to come to terms with expressions arising from another time, history, and culture. But there is much in the psalms that is profoundly human and thus universal. It is as well to start by focusing attention on the lines that speak most to us. Take time to study and reflect on those lines that are more dissonant; coming to grips with what is disturbing can be a source of deeper understanding and even enlightenment.

Reading

A short reading from scripture may be taken from the lectionary or the liturgy of the day or chosen for a specific concern of the group.

Responsory

The responsory that follows the reading gives the group an opportunity to assimilate and affirm the reading to which it has just listened.

Gospel Canticle

Both Morning and Evening Prayer have as their climax a New Testament canticle specifically celebrating the revelation of Jesus Christ. At Morning Prayer it is the canticle of Zechariah, or the Benedictus (Luke 1:68–79)°; for Evening Prayer the canticle of Mary, or the Magnificat (Luke 1:46–55).† These are recited in the same way as the psalms. Since the canticle is the same every day, a group that recites the office regularly can learn to chant it.

Closing Prayers

These may include intercessions from the group, followed by the Lord's Prayer and a closing prayer appropriate to the day or season. The entire office is concluded by a blessing and dismissal.

°See pages 74-75.
†See pages 72-73.

Antiphons

The antiphon is a short statement, taken from the psalm itself or from the liturgy of the season, which is recited at the beginning and end of each psalm or canticle. The antiphon can often be the key to the meditation on the psalm. When it can be sung, it greatly enhances the beauty and variety of the prayer. Many of the psalms and accompanying antiphons have been set to music; Joseph Gelineau's collection is perhaps the best known (*Thirty Psalms and Two Canticles*, World Library of Sacred Music, 1957). While, not surprisingly, some of the language used is sexist, the musical settings are quite lovely and will add considerably to the worship experience.

A Service of Lauds

All: Send forth your Spirit, and they shall be created, and you shall renew the face of the earth, alleluia, alleluia!

Cantor: O Lord, open my lips.

All: And my mouth shall proclaim your praise.

Cantor: In the morning we are filled with your mercy.

All: We rejoice and are delighted.

(Short time of silent prayer)

THE HYMN

THE PSALMS

Monday: Psalms 29 and 47
Antiphon: O Lord, our Lord, how wonderful is your name in all the earth, alleluia, alleluia!

Tuesday: Psalms 67 and 96
Antiphon: Sing joyfully to the Lord, all you lands, serve the Lord with gladness.

Wednesday: Psalms 97 and 146
Antiphon: Faithfulness shall spring from the earth, and justice look down from heaven.

Thursday: Canticle of Hannah (1 Samuel 2:1–10), Psalm 98
Antiphon: O Lord, you have broken my bonds; I will offer sacrifice of praise.

Friday: Psalms 51 and 84
Antiphon: Have mercy on me, O Lord, according to your great mercy.

Saturday: Psalm 116 (114–115°), I and II
Antiphon: How can I repay you, God, for your goodness to me? I will take the cup of salvation, I will call on your name.

Sunday: Psalms 63 and 118
Antiphon: All the ends of the earth have seen the salvation of our God, alleluia!

THE READING

RESPONSORY TO THE READING
Monday
Cantor: Lord, you give strength to your people, you bless your people with peace.
All: Lord, you give strength to your people, you bless your people with peace.
Cantor: You sit as ruler forever.
All: You bless your people with peace.
Cantor: Glory and power are yours, O God.
All: Lord, you give strength to your people, you bless your people with peace.

Tuesday
Cantor: O God, be gracious and bless us, and let your face send its light upon us. *(All repeat.)*
Let all the peoples praise you, O God. *(All:)* And let your face send its light upon us.
Give glory to God, who comes to rule the earth. *(All repeat first line.)*

Wednesday
Cantor: It is the Lord who keeps faith forever, who is just to those who are oppressed. *(All repeat.)*

°Based on the Septuagint, the Vulgate and all English versions derived from it use an alternate numbering.

Happy are they whose hope is in the Lord. *(All:)* who is just to those who are oppressed. I will praise the Lord all my days. *(All repeat first line.)*

Thursday

Cantor: You lift up the lowly from the dust, from the dungheap you raise the poor. *(All repeat.)* You guard the steps of the faithful. *(All:)* From the dungheap you raise the poor. My heart exults in the Lord. *(All repeat first line.)*

Friday

Cantor: A pure heart create for me, O God, put a steadfast spirit within me. *(All repeat.)* Turn away your face from my sins. *(All:)* Put a steadfast spirit within me. My tongue rings out your goodness, O God. *(All repeat first line.)*

Saturday

Cantor: How gracious is the Lord, and just; our God has compassion. *(All repeat.)* The Lord protects the simple hearts. *(All:)* Our God has compassion. I call on the name of the Lord with thanksgiving. *(All repeat first line.)*

Sunday

Cantor: My soul shall be filled as with a banquet, my mouth shall praise you with joy. *(All repeat.)* Your love is better than life. *(All:)* My mouth shall praise you with joy. In your name, O God, I lift up my hands. *(All repeat first line.)*

THE BENEDICTUS (The Song of Zechariah)

THE PRAYERS
Intercessions From the Group
The Lord's Prayer
Collect *(chosen by leader)*

THE DISMISSAL

Cantor: May the peace of the Lord be always with us.
All: And with those who are absent from us. Amen.

Service of Worship Based on the Poem "For the Unknown Goddess" by Elizabeth Brewster*

GREETING   (The gathered group exchanges words and signs of peace.)

INVOKING THE POWER OF THE GODDESS

PRAYER OF CONFESSION   (A unison prayer expressing ways we participate in our own oppression by not claiming the power of being.)

COMMUNAL STATEMENT OF ACCEPTANCE AND PARDON

SILENCE

READING THE POEM

A RITUAL RESPONSE   (Lying on the floor to listen to the humming in our cells; a walk outside to become aware of the earth; a meditation, repeating phrases, noting emotions evoked by the poem, etc.)

AN INTERPRETATION OF THE POEM AND TESTIFYING ABOUT EXPERIENCES OF BEING AND NONBEING

SILENCE

PRAYERS   (For ourselves
For people who help us claim the power of being
For the strengthening of our faith
For the power to create being in other people)

*See pages 69-70.

BLESSING RITUAL   *(The women turn to one another and ask for words and signs of blessing. This may be done individually or collectively, such as the laying on of hands.)*

Rituals

Closing Ritual: "Image-breaking/Image-building" Workshop

Search for the Lost Coin
The community gathers outside the chapel. A flute player stands at the far end of the entryway. A singer stands at the door. The flute plays the melody of the song "Never Touch a Singing Bird" by Malvina Reynolds. The singer sings the song alone, and the community repeats it as they enter the chapel.

> Never touch a singing bird, a wild bird.
> Never move or say a word,
>   But sit and listen quietly,
>   Underneath the forest tree.
> You cannot catch and hold her song,
> For if it's tame, it's not the same.
> The singing bird does not belong
>   To you or me or anyone.
>   Or anyone,
> This bird won't sing unless she's free.[3]

At the end of the song a reader standing in the middle of the chapel reads the parable of the lost coin (Luke 15:8–10) and asks the group to enter to seek the lost coin. The community gathers in a circle just below the platform.

A woman speaks: "We begin the search for the tenth coin by honoring gifts of the nine which remain. If you wish, share the strengths of your tradition that provide meaning for you and lead you to seek the tenth coin." She then steps to the altar and lights the nine candles. The sharing begins. At the end of the sharing, a litany is read by all.°

°See pages 60-61.

Dancers then interpret the poem "God's Birthdance" by David Wilson, inviting the community to join in at the end of the dance.* At the conclusion of the dancing the community returns to the circle, is seated, and pauses for a time of silent meditation.

A reader reads Genesis 1:27.

Small candles, signifying the tenth coin, are passed among the community. One woman lights her candle from the nine candles on the altar and begins to light the other candles. When the candles are all lit they are placed in the cinder box in the center of the circle. Each woman returns to her place and takes the hands of the women next to her. There is a moment of silence as the light from all the "tenth coins" blazes forth as one in the midst of the community.

The round "Joy Shall Come" is sung.

Joy shall come even to the wilderness, and the parched land shall
    then know great gladness;
As the rose, as the rose shall deserts blossom, deserts like a garden
    blossom.
For living springs shall give cool water, in the desert streams
    shall flow,
For living springs shall give cool water, in the desert streams
    shall flow.[4]

At the conclusion of the song each woman picks up a lighted candle, blows it out, and leaves with it. The candle is hers to take back to her own community as a reminder of this place, this time, and the support of her sisters in her search for the lost coin.†

---

*See pages 77-81.

†This ritual was planned by everyone who took part in the week and reflects themes, images, and concerns that became part of the collective experience. The opening song was chosen because one participant had made a striking comparison of spiritual search with the sound of a bird singing in the forest—as soon as one approaches the sound, the bird moves farther away, never to be caught or even fully seen. The theme of the lost coin and the acknowledgment of the nine that were not lost represent some of the tension participants felt between wishing to keep what meant most to them from the past and wanting to leave the past in search of the new.

A Ritual Meal

A meal celebrated in this way is an occasion for a deeply meditative experience of food, environment, and other persons. Derived from Chinese Buddhist tradition,[5] its emphasis is on simplicity, beauty, and awareness. The pace is unhurried. The formal elements create an atmosphere of peacefulness which frees the attention for savoring all aspects of the experience. It is carried out in silence except for the time of sharing at the end, and it is suitable for large or small groups.

The general plan. Ask participants to gather for an introduction about a half hour before the meal is to begin. Explain at this time what is to happen so that they will be at ease and so that no further verbal directions will be necessary.

Point out that the food is to be savored, and invite participants to use the pencil and paper they will find at their places to write down whatever they observe of the taste, smell, and texture of the food, as well as what they see in the surroundings. Other reflections, even poems, may come to mind during the course of the meal. Encourage them to jot these down as well.

Ask each person to spend the next twenty minutes in a silent meditative walk, preferably out of doors, observing her surroundings. Invite each one to select during that time a natural object (stone, weed, twig) that appeals to her and to bring it with her to the meal.

Ring a bell when the time is up so all can enter the dining room together.

The setting. The room in which the meal is to take place should be as simple, peaceful, and beautiful as possible. Natural wood floors, windows, and uncluttered walls are good to look for. Remove unnecessary furniture.

The meal is eaten sitting on the floor. (Stools and low tables may be provided for those who cannot sit on the floor.) Each person has a cushion with a place mat in front of it. The place mat is set with plate, cup, and eating utensils. Cushions and place mats are arranged in a square, an open rectangle, or whatever pattern works best with the shape of the room. The arrangement should be pleasing to the eye and should allow room for servers to pass comfortably with the dishes. Place a pencil and some paper at each place setting. Simple arrangements of fresh flowers or leaves may be placed where participants may see them easily.

The menu. Food should be simple, delicious, attractive, and easily served and eaten. A sample menu might be: First course: homemade soup or broth; second course: rice and vegetable or meat casserole, bean or tossed salad, herb tea; third course: gelatin or cream dessert with fresh fruit, or dried fruits and nuts.

Serving. Each person is served individually by servers chosen from among the participants. The server carries sufficient food on a tray to serve six to eight persons for the course. Since participants are sitting on the floor, the server kneels down to be at their height and greets each person respectfully (nonverbally, of course). As the person takes the food, the server responds nonverbally with an acknowledgment of respect and thanks. The server should take time to eat her own food before proceeding to serve the next course (or second helpings of the main dish and beverage). It is usually not necessary to clear until the meal is over.

Sharing. When all have finished eating there may be a time of sharing. Participants may show the objects selected during their walk, explaining what appeal or meaning the objects had for them, or they may read or recount observations or reflections jotted down during the meal or provoked by the total experience. The sharing may conclude with a reading, a prayer, or a piece of recorded music.

To take care of cleaning up afterward, it may be well to give a signal for all to rise, greet one another, and then work together in a peaceful manner to wash the dishes and restore the room to its original condition.

A Woman's Ritual

This ritual was used at Grailville as part of the "Image-breaking/Image-building" workshop. The basis for the ritual is found in "Women Welcome the Equinox" in *Womanspirit*.[6] It was freely adapted from that material and from parts of the Eleusinian Mysteries and the myth of Demeter, the goddess of agriculture and the fruitfulness of humankind. The following is the text and a description of the various ritual acts.

The space—the Oratory at Grailville—had been cleared of everything that moved, including the huge cross that hung behind the altar. A large vase of wheat shafts stood in front of the altar. To the left of the altar was a container filled with sand and cinders. This served as a place to put the lighted tapers at the end of the ritual. One large lighted candle was on the altar.

The leader introduced the ritual:

"In a series of rituals—as a group—we will enact the myth of Demeter and Persephone: (1) The rape of Persephone and Demeter's search for her; (2) The greeting and cheering of Demeter at Eleusis; (3) The reuniting of mother and daughter; (4) The renewal of the land.

"This is the story of Demeter, the grain-mother, and Persephone, her daughter, the Queen of Hades. The worship of Demeter and Persephone formed the center of the Eleusinian Mysteries.

"One lovely day when Persephone, the daughter of Demeter, was gathering flowers with some of her companions, Hades, the god of the underworld, abducted her. The loss of Persephone was unbearable to Demeter, and so she went wandering over the face of the earth for nine days, unable to eat or to drink. Finally Hecate advised her to ask Helios directly concerning Persephone's whereabouts, and Demeter did so. But the truth was doubly heartrending for her. Demeter therefore left the home of the gods and continued wandering, taking on the appearance of an old woman.

"By and by Demeter made the acquaintance of a couple who had a newborn son, Demophoon. She became their servant, and the child's nurse. Demophoon flourished under her care, and Demeter was intent upon making him into a god. His mother came upon her just as she was about to burn away his mortal parts, however, and screamed so loudly that the spell was broken and Demeter went wandering once again.

"So disconsolate was the grain-mother on account of these events that she refused to allow the earth to bring forth fruit until Persephone was returned to her. Drought and famine came over the land. Finally two nymphs decided to confess what they knew to Demeter. One produced the girdle Persephone had dropped when she was abducted; the other reported that she had actually seen Persephone looking unhappy, but very much a queen.

"At length Zeus sent Iris and the other gods and goddesses to beg Demeter for relief from the famine, but even then she would not be moved. Nothing but the return of Persephone would do. Finally, Zeus ordered Hades to return the girl, and Hades didn't dare disobey him. He did, however, secretly slip a pomegranate seed into Persephone's mouth, thus forcing her to return to his underground kingdom once a year. Hermes then took Persephone back to the upper world in his chariot, and the reunion of mother and daughter was moving to behold.

"Demeter was, of course, saddened to realize that Persephone must spend a third of every year in the underworld because of eating the pomegranate seed. For this reason Demeter created the season of winter. Nonetheless there was great rejoicing at the reunion of mother and daughter, and Demeter and Persephone returned to Olympus with the other immortals."[7]

1. & 2. The Rape of Persephone and Demeter's Search and The Greeting and Cheering of Demeter at Eleusis
The leader gave the following instructions:
"Take a lighted candle and wander outside with it. At a certain point blow out the candle. Then begin wandering again, thinking perhaps of the meaning of the loss of the light, the separation of mother and daughter, the loss of the fertility of the earth.

"A bell will sound for us to regather here in the Oratory. As you enter, take a sip of barley water from the cup that sustained Demeter and gather around the platform to take part in the jesting that cheered Demeter."
The women stood. One woman lit her candle from the large candle on the altar and then began to light the candles the other women held. Everyone then left the room and wandered around the fields with the candles. The large candle on the altar was extinguished. At the bell, the women returned and entered the

Oratory. Two women held cups with barley water gruel in them which each woman drank. They then gathered in a circle. Two women began skits and clowning: at first they worked between themselves and then got the rest of the group to make sculptures. This particular part of the evening ended with the reading of a poem and the relighting of the large candle on the altar.

Thaw[8]

No matter how long the Winter is
Thaw comes
season by season
we learn this
too slowly

No matter how long we have spent
wrapped in a frozen season
no matter how deep under the snow
the private grief lies
one day . . .
thaw comes

we are never prepared for it

and what was once safe for our feet
changes
water released from ice and mud and madness
and we open our eyes to
earth-shift, stone-change

everything thawing
thawing like a madness
the earth opening
water running

and all of our secrets
exposed.

—Martha Courtot

3. The Reuniting of Mother and Daughter

The leader spoke:

"Let us unite with the rejoicing of Demeter and Persephone by recalling those times in our lives when we have found light and joy working and playing with women. If you wish, come up, relight your candle from the large candle on the altar, and place it in this box to signify that light and joy. And again, if you wish, you may share that light and joy with the rest of the group."

The women came up one by one, lit their candles, and placed them in the box. Most of them then spoke a few words of explanation or invoked the names of women that were important to them. At the end, everyone stood in a circle of silence.

4. The Renewal of the Land

To begin the final ritual in this series of rituals, the leader said:

"With the return of Persephone came the renewal of the land. Take these seeds of corn as a symbol of the renewal of our own lives, the lives of other women we know, and our dedication to the renewal of our mother the earth."

The leader then led the group out of the Oratory to the edge of a field. She threw her handful of seeds over the fence into the field. The others followed suit.

Ritual for Saying Good-bye

This is a good-bye for members of a group that has been together for some time and is now disbanding. The ritual as given below was designed for use out-of-doors. If outdoor space is not available, participants should be asked to bring appropriate materials (colored paper, paste, string, yarn, beads, natural objects, etc.) to the site of the ritual.

Members of the group gather together and stand while a leader reads the Navaho Blessing:

> God is before us.
> God is behind us.
> God is above us.
> God is below us.

God's words shall come from our mouths
For we are God's essence, a sign of God's love.

All is finished in beauty.
All is finished in beauty.
All is finished in beauty.
All is finished in beauty.[9]

At the conclusion of the reading, the group spreads out and each member finds a place that belongs to her. Then each participant finds an object or makes out of materials available something that represents her or what she brings to the group or leaves with the group as she departs.

When everyone has her object, the group gathers together again and forms a circle around the objects. Then all read together the first six lines of the Navaho Blessing.

After the reading, everyone takes hands and moves in a circle to the right, saying, "Love is like a ring, a ring that has no ending." After circling a couple of times, change directions and circle to the left, still chanting. When the motion comes to an end, everyone drops hands and picks up one of the objects. Then the group reads together the last four lines of the blessing.

Finally, the participants leave the circle and return to the spaces they found for themselves at the start of the ritual. The leader concludes with a reading of the last four lines of the blessing.

Ritual for Ending a Close Relationship
This ritual is for two persons who have been closely connected through partnership in work, keeping a home together, or some other alliance and are ending this phase of their relationship. Both persons have been and will continue to be members of a community such as a group of close mutual friends or a church.

The meaning of the event:
   a. There has been a mutual bond, a union, between two individuals.
   b. They are choosing to end the relationship.

c. Each will continue her life as an individual, but in a new way. They will, in a sense, be new persons in their community.

d. The community may experience grief over the loss of that unique relationship and frustration at having to relate to each person in a new way.

The ritual. The community forms a circle, holding hands. The two ending the relationship are part of the circle but do not stand next to each other. Each of these two brings a piece of cloth and a needle and yarn. They enter the center of the circle and sew together the separate pieces of cloth. They then either pull the yarn loose to separate the cloth or rip it apart. They say the following words to the community: "Our life together has happened within the context of this community. We ask that you struggle with us as we come to you in a new way."

Each of the two then goes to each member of the group and requests verbally or nonverbally the kind of support or affirmation they would like. The group member responds to the request and also says, "Be whole, alone and with us."

The two rejoin the circle. Words of hope may be read by a group member to strengthen the individuals and the community. The ritual concludes with a song that is important to the life of the community.

A Fiftieth Birthday Celebration

Given: The fiftieth birthday of a woman who has been family oriented and active in church. Her husband and three children are present.

Elements in the celebration (ideas and feelings): Celebration of a birthday; the opportunity for new directions in growth; thanks for gifts (talents) given; respect for age/maturity; realization of one's own limits; community/family sense; sense of freedom and autonomy.

Setting: Fellowship hall of church; family and invited friends; seating in a comfortable circle; table in center of circle covered with robe *(see below)* then with flowers in all stages of growth (seeds, buds, full blossoms, fading blooms).

The Celebration. With the community seated, the family escorts the woman into the hall while all sing "Happy Birthday." The host or hostess introduces the woman and invites her to remember out loud highlights of her life.

The community then joins in the remembrance and gives thanks for the gifts of this particular person.

The family then engages in remembrance and gift-giving, ending with "You gave me a seed, I planted and harvested; now here are new seeds to be planted."

Someone reads or summarizes a story about nature that emphasizes death and resurrection (past life and present life), such as *Hope for the Flowers* by Trina Paulus.[10] The story may be interpreted in dance. The community responds with "Life is changed, not taken away." The dancer then passes out flowers from the table, and the husband gives the woman the robe symbolizing her butterfly wings. She puts it on and is led into the center of a line dance° which forms around her like a cocoon. The woman then breaks through the "cocoon" and leads the community into the reception room nearby while all sing "Happy Birthday" again.

Ritual of Saying Good-bye to a Dying Person

This ritual assumes that both the dying person and that person's family and friends have come to some acceptance of death as imminent. The following lists of purposes, feelings, reactions, etc. can serve as background material for the ritual.

Why a ritual of saying good-bye to someone who is dying?
>To help the person say good-bye to the community
>To help the community to say good-bye to the person
>To bring a sense of bondedness after death
>To affirm the life that has been

Our Feelings
>—Possessiveness, not wanting to give up the person
>—Anger
>—Grief
>—Relief of pain and stress
>—Guilt, denial

°Use music familiar to the community.

Our Body Actions
- —Awkwardness, head bowed, silence, crying, weakness, confusion
- —Loss of words, touching or not touching the dying person
- —Cowering, cracking jokes (distraction from grief)
- —Drunkenness, flippancy
- —Oversolicitude
- —Busyness

Traditional Reactions
- —Helplessness and wailing (catharsis), somberness
- —Favorite hymns, prayers, drums, songs
- —Getting on with the business of life

The Dying Person's Needs
- —To say good-bye
- —To say special things to members of the family and friends, individually and corporately
- —To be relieved of guilt feelings

The Needs of Family and Friends
- —Time with the dying person
- —Reconciliation, forgiveness
- —To let the dying person know that they will be missed, that their space will not be totally filled, and that life will not collapse after their death

Words to Reinforce the Action
- —Words of comfort
- —Words of support
- —Words of encouragement to express feelings and to deal with them directly.

What Can Be Done Corporately
- —Time for silence/meditation
- —Time for spoken prayer
- —Remembering
- —Photographs, tapes
- —Favorite foods
- —Family stories
- —Singing

The ritual leader is the facilitator who brings together the community and the dying person. The dying person discusses what she or he would like to come from the ritual, who is to be included (perhaps doctors, nurses, or other patients that have become close), and the length of the ritual. The community (friends and family) talk about what they would like from the time too. Everyone is asked to bring something such as food, a favorite item, or pictures to the ritual. It is important to give everyone verbal permission to feel what they need to feel and to ask for help if they need it.

The order of elements in the ritual we designed is as follows:
1. Call together, introductory words
2. Share memories, recall good times and happy events, use of photographs, etc.
3. Individual time with the person and community time
4. Reflective time, quiet or verbal prayer and meditation, holding hands
5. Singing or listening to favorite songs, music, instruments
6. Eating together

This ritual need not take place all on one day.

Prayers, Confessions, Litanies

A Litany[11]

O God of a thousand names and faces,
    Teach us to know and love you.
Mother and father of all life on earth,
    Teach us to know and love you.
You who live in the cells of all life,
    Teach us to know and love you.
Lady of peace, of love, of wisdom,
    Teach us to know and love you.
Lord of all the stars and planets,
    Teach us to know and love you.
Best consoler, inward guest,
    Teach us to know and love you.

Giver of gifts and light of our hearts,
  Teach us to know and love you.
Fill the inmost depths of our hearts,
  And teach us to know and love you.
Wash what is soiled, heal what is wounded,
  And teach us to know and love you.
Bend what is rigid, warm what is frigid,
  And teach us to know and love you.
Restore to us our humanness,
  And teach us to know and love you.

—Sharon Owens

To the Goddess[12]

Let me know thee better
O cradle of my youth,
Source of my plenty,
Cool wooded retreat for my sorrow
and soft bed for my final sleep—
my first and last Mother.

—Catherine A. Callaghan

Eternal Spirit of God, who exists in the humming cells of my body, as well as beyond the chaos of the universe, I want to experience your power in my life, I want to feel your healing in my hurts, I want to know your love in my relationships. Take me into your caring arms and push me forward into new life, each day and all days, forevermore. Amen.

—Estelle Petitt[13]

O God, You who have always been our teacher,
our guide, our shelter.
With the power of *your* future, break this
community open to your light, your life,
and new ways of loving and caring for each other
So that—thy will be done. Amen.

—Margaret Purdy, Canada[14]

O Mother and Father of us all, you who bring the poles of our experience into relation, have pity on us in our divisions. Grant to the communities to which I belong—The Grail, the Christian church, the United States of America, and to all the broken communities of the world, the strength to recognize our differences and the wisdom to use them well in the building up of the whole human community. We ask this in the name of Jesus, the Christ, who is our brother and sister now and forever. Amen.

—Marian Ronan

One who is with us in all our searching—

Help us to build a world which allows all
people to get in touch with the lost parts
of their humanity.

Help the boy who is afraid to be gentle
        the girl who is afraid to dare
        the man who only knows how to work
        the woman whose fortune is her face.

Help us to be open to others in their searching.
O God, sustain us on our journey.

—Phyllis Kuestner[15]

From whence cometh my help?
        My help cometh from God-within-me;
        My help cometh from God-within-you;

In calmness, in silence,
        in serenity, peace envelops me;

My life's force must be sustained—
        the meeting glance,
            the word unspoken,
                the touch,
                    the warmth of friends—
                must feed my soul.

—Bernice Smith[16]

From the teachings of the church which have oppressed and limited the lives of women, denying us the abundance of life and spirit promised in Jesus Christ,
O God, save us.
We have allowed ourselves to be defined by others' expectations of us; we have believed the myths and lies that the culture has told about us,
O God, forgive us.
For the times when we have discounted our dreams, our visions, our insights, when we have not taken ourselves or our gifts seriously but have hidden them under a bushel,
O God, forgive us.
For the systematic execution of women who were called witches, women who did not fit an image of the proper woman,
O God, have mercy.
For the times we have turned away from our sisters, denying our common sisterhood and common experience,
O God, forgive us.
For the times in our silence or in our very words we have been complicit in affirming the structures and practices which deny us and our sisters our heritage and our calling,
O God, forgive us.

—Marie Fortune[17]

Confession[18]

Leader 1: We know ourselves to be a people who distort sexuality.

All: We are separated from ourselves, each other, and the God of Life.

Leader 2: Let us confess our brokenness.

Women: As women caught in our tradition, we confess that we have helped perpetuate the myth of feminine inferiority by adopting the role of natural followers.

Men: As men caught in our tradition, we confess that we have helped perpetuate the myth of masculine superiority by assuming the role of natural leaders.

Women: As women, we confess that we have been willing to

limit our image to that of wives, mothers, and sexual objects for men.

Men: As men, we confess that we have often seen women as sexual objects. We have been a part of restricting their roles to those of wives and mothers.

Women: We confess that we have not sought our own real identity in scripture and history. We have failed to trust ourselves and other women. We have often been our own worst enemies.

Men: We confess that we have perpetuated religious teachings which reinforce illusions of male supremacy. While we exalt servanthood, we leave the menial tasks to women.

Women: We confess that we have participated in a system which inhibits and denies self-affirmation and creativity to all sorts and conditions of persons.

Men: We confess that we have paid lip service to universal equality, yet our lives are based on sexual discrimination and, in fact, we have placed women in subordinate positions.

All: Moved by the power of the Holy Spirit, we accuse ourselves because we have not allowed God to form us as a new people. We confess our sin to God, to the church, and to the world. We pledge to work for reconciliation with one another.

Leader 1: In the name of our Creator, our Redeemer, our Comforter, you are forgiven. You are freed from the past and its oppression. You are free to move to a new future of mutuality and love, taking into account the sins of the past and not bound by them. The gift is complete; live in the grace of God's love.

Psalm 137: An Interpretation[19]

Reader 1: By the waters of Babylon . . .

Reader 2: Babylon, land of forced exile, of powerlessness.
Babylon, being enslaved by another people.
There is no control.

Reader 3: Babylon, living in powerlessness,
Terrorized in our homes and on the streets,
In the media and in education:
The bedrooms, the newspapers, the cars, the shopping centers.
Babylon, our work is for others and not for ourselves.
There is no control.

Reader 1: There we sat down and wept, when we remembered Zion . . .

Reader 2: Weeping for our remembered home, our faith, our way of living.
Weeping for the lost freedom of our people.

Reader 3: Weeping for the home we have never had.
Weeping because of our oppression,
Because of the violence against our bodies, our minds, and our spirits.
Weeping for the hope of freedom for our kind.

Reader 1: On the willows there we hung up our lyres.
For there our captors required of us songs,
And our tormentors, mirth,
Saying, "Sing us one of the songs of Zion!"

Reader 2: The Babylonians would exploit the expressions of our faith, our hymns, our prayers.
Our captors would rob us of our lullabies, the poetry, art, and all the creativeness of our people,
The best of our thinking.
Our tormentors would have us dance and sing for them rather than for Yahweh.
They would have us laugh.

Reader 3: The Patriarchs would program the expressions of our being and faith:
"God is Father, Son, and Holy Ghost . . ."
"All men are created equal . . ."
They have allowed us no songs, no prayers,
And we have sung their songs with full voice.
Our husbands, our fathers, our lovers, our brothers, uncles, and cousins use our bodies for their pleasure and their progeny.

They use our love and gentleness to oppress us,

They stifle our creativeness, the best of our thinking.

For the love and favors of our oppressors,

And for lack of love for ourselves, we do not resist.

Reader 3: Our oppressors put their feet on our necks by building pedestals and whorehouses,

Insulting, beating, and raping us.

They ask if we enjoy it.

Reader 1: On the willows there we hung up our lyres.

For how shall we sing the Lord's song in a foreign
land?

Reader 2: No! We cannot and will not go against our tradition,
our faith,

We cannot accept the injustices to our people and our
children.

No! We cannot break our covenant with God.

Reader 3: No! We cannot and will not settle for traditional definitions of who we are and how we are to act.

We will not prostitute ourselves for money, for secu-
rity, for the approval of our oppressors.

We cannot accept the injustices to ourselves, our sisters, and our children.

No! We cannot deny our faith and vision for the
future.

Reader 1: How shall we sing the Lord's song in a foreign land?

If I forget you, O Jerusalem, let my right hand
wither!

Reader 2: We must keep the covenant with Yahweh.

How can we remember our home, our faith, our way
of living while in exile?

How will our children learn the ways of justice?

Reader 3: We must carry on the struggle of our sisters before
us.

But how can we sing our own song

When we have no voice,

When our voices are not heard.

When we speak in the words of our captors,

When we have no words of our own.

How will we and our children learn the ways of
 justice.

Reader 1: Let my tongue cleave to the roof of my mouth,
If I do not remember you,
If I do not set Jerusalem above my highest joy!

Reader 2: Take away our tongues if we do not sing and
 proclaim
the faith of our ancestors,
the trust that we are not abandoned,
the longing for our homes.
May we remain prisoners, if we relax in our captivity
and acquiesce to our oppressors,
If we do not remember Jerusalem, our home, and
Yahweh, our God, above all else,
May we perish in exile.

Reader 3: Take away our voices if we do not give voice
to the truth of our past,
the reality of our present,
and the hope of our future.
May we remain victims, if we relax in our captivity
and acquiesce to our oppressors.
If we do not remember into the future the home we
have never had.
May we remain isolated in the homes of others.

—Gail Burress
Amelie Ratcliff
Liz Shellberg

Wisdom Herself Speaks[20]
(Adapted from Proverbs 8:22–31)

I-am-was-will-be for all time, eternally begotten from the
 beginning of time, the first of the acts of creation.
Ages ago, I was set up, at the first, before the beginning of the
 earth.
When there were no depths, I was brought forth, when there
 were no springs abounding with water.

Before the mountains had been shaped, before the hills, I was
  brought forth;
Before the creation of the earth with its fields, or the
  beginning of the dust of the world,
When the heavens were established, I was there, when a circle
  appeared on the face of the deep,
When the skies became firm above, when the fountains burst
  forth from the deep,
When the sea was assigned its limit, so that the waters might
  not exceed their boundaries,
When the foundations of the earth took shape, then I was
  present like a partner to a master worker.
And I was daily a delight, rejoicing always in creation,
Rejoicing in the inhabited world and delighting in its sons and
  daughters.

—Estelle Petitt
Catherine A. Callaghan

The Ninety-nine Names of God

(This resource list can be used in the activity on page 19 and in
any prayers, confessions, and litanies.)

Mother of My Heart	Power	Encompasser
Searcher	O Song	Opener
Blossom of All Things	Laughter	Center of Fire
Clown	Mover	My Fire
Gentle Trickster	Becoming	The Hang Loose One
The Great Cry	The Putterer	Listener
Whole of All	Earth	Spreader
Surroundance	Bonfire	Sanctuary
Hearth	Life-force	Delight
Dancing Energy	Wonder	Mother
Tears	Play	Cosmos
Presence	Lover	Safety
Heat	Tenderness	Holder
Desire	Anger	Healing
The Compassionate Womb	Sufferer	Light
Quieter	Breath	Upsetter

Face	Color	Regard
Word	Passion	O Heart
Strength	Outsidedness	Flowering
Withinness	Wind	Matrix
Sound	Mourner	Silence
Voice of Trumpets	Dear Child	Fire
Control	Essence	Justice
Relief	Candor	Rejoicing
Sigh	Companion	Ocean
The Dance	Renewer	Simplicity
Grandmother	Nameless	Giver and Taker
Wholeness	The Caller	Uncertainty
The Undemanding	Anxiety	The Ever Returning
O Dream	Home	Child of the Cosmos
Air	Warm Center	Womb of All
O Shore	Sky	Singer
Sister	Comforter	Dear Friend

Poems

For the Unknown Goddess[21]

Lady, the unknown goddess,
we have prayed long enough only
To Yahweh the thunder god.

Now we should pray to you again
goddess of a thousand names and faces
Ceres Venus Demeter Isis
Ianna Queen of Heaven
or by whatever name
you would be known

you who sprang from the sea
who are present in the moisture of love
who live in the humming cells
of all life
who are rain
with its million soft fingers

and you who are earth
you with your beautiful ruined face
wrinkled by all
that your children have done to you.

sunlike lady
crowned with the whirling planets.

Lady of peace, of good counsel,
of love, of wisdom

we invoke your name
which we no longer know

and pray to you
to restore our humanity
as we restore your divinity.

—Elizabeth Brewster

Bakerwoman God[22]

Bakerwoman God,
I am your living bread.
Strong, brown, Bakerwoman God,
I am your low, soft, and being-
shaped loaf.
I am your rising
bread, well-kneaded
by some divine and knotty
pair of knuckles, by your warm
earth-hands.
I am bread well-kneaded.

Put me in fire, Bakerwoman God,
put me in your own bright fire.

I am warm, warm as you
from fire, I am white

and gold, soft and hard,
brown and round.
I am so warm from fire.

Break me, Bakerwoman God!
I am broken under your caring Word.
Drop me in your special juice in pieces.
Drop me in your blood.
Drunken me in the great red flood.
Self-giving chalice, swallow me.
My skin shines in the divine wine.
My face is cup-covered and I drown.

I fall up
in a red pool
in a gold world
where your warm
sunskin hand is there
to catch and hold me.
Bakerwoman God, remake me.

—Alla Bozarth-Campbell

Veni Sancte Spiritus[23]

Come, Holy Spirit,
And send from heaven
A ray of your light.

Come, Parent of the poor,
Come, Giver of gifts,
Come, Light of hearts.

Best Consoler,
Sweet Guest of the soul,
Sweet Refreshment.

In labor, rest,
In heat, coolness,
In grief, comfort.

O most blessed Light,
Fill the intimate depths
Of the hearts of your faithful.

Without your power
We are empty
And open to harm.

Wash what is unclean,
Water what is dried out,
Heal whoever is wounded.

Bend what is rigid,
Warm what is frigid,
Rule what is wayward.

Give to your faithful
Confidence in you,
Give your seven holy gifts.

Give the merit of virtue,
Give salvation at death,
Give perennial joy.

Amen. Alleluia.

Magnificat[24]

My soul proclaims your greatness, O my God,
and my spirit has rejoiced in you, my Savior,

For your regard has blessed me,
poor, and a serving woman.

From this day all generations
will call me blessed,

For you, who are mighty, have made me great.
Most Holy be your Name.

Your mercy is on those who fear you
throughout all generations.

You have showed strength with your arm.
You have scattered the proud in their hearts' fantasy.

You have put down the mighty from their seat,
and have lifted up the powerless.

You have filled the hungry with good things,
and have sent the rich away empty.

You, remembering your mercy,
have helped your people Israel—

As you promised Abraham and Sarah.
Mercy to their children, forever.

Meditation on Luke 1^{25}

It is written that mary said
my soul doth magnify the lord
and my spirit hath rejoiced in god my savior
for he hath regarded the low estate of his handmaiden
for behold from henceforth
all generations shall call me blessed

Today we express that differently
my soul sees the land of freedom
my spirit will leave anxiety behind
the empty faces of women will be filled with life
we will become human beings
long awaited by the generations sacrificed before us

It is written that mary said
for he that is mighty hath done to me great things
and holy is his name
and his mercy is on them that fear him
from generation to generation

Today we express that differently
we shall dispossess our owners and we shall laugh
at those who claim to understand feminine nature
the rule of males over females will end
objects will become subjects
they will achieve their own better right

It is written that mary said
he hath shewed strength with his arm
he hath scattered the proud
he hath put down the mighty from their seats
and exalted them of low degree

Today we express that differently
we shall dispossess our owners and we shall laugh
at those who claim to understand feminine nature
the rule of males over females will end
objects will become subjects
they will achieve their own better right

It is written that mary said
he hath filled the hungry with good things
and the rich he hath sent empty away
he hath holpen his servant israel
in remembrance of his mercy.

Today we express that differently
women will go to the moon and sit in parliaments
their desire for self-determination will be fulfilled
the craving for power will go unheeded
their fears will be unnecessary
and exploitation will come to an end.

—Dorothee Soelle

The Song of Zechariah (Luke 1:68–79)[26]

Blessed be the great God of Israel,
   who has visited and redeemed this people,

And has raised up a horn of salvation for us
   in this royal house,
As was spoken by the mouths
   of the holy prophets from of old,
That we should be saved
   from our enemies,
And from the hand
   of all who hate us;
To perform the mercy
   promised to our ancestors,
And to remember
   God's holy covenant,
The covenant sworn to Abraham
   and Sarah, our parents;
To grant that we, being delivered
   from the hands of our enemies,
Might serve God without fear
In holiness and righteousness
   all the days of our lives.

And you, child, will be called
   the prophet of the Most High,
For you will go before the Holy One
   to prepare the way;
To give knowledge of salvation to God's people
   in the forgiveness of their sins,
Through the tender mercy of our God,
When the day shall dawn upon us
   from on high;
To give light to those who sit
   in darkness and in the shadow of death;
To guide our feet
   into the way of peace.

Crossing a Creek[27]

   crossing a creek
   requires 3 things:

a certain serenity of mind
bare feet
and a sure trust
that the snake we know
slides silently
underwater
just beyond our vision
will choose to ignore
the flesh
that cuts through
its territory
and we *will* pass through

some people think crossing a creek
is easy
but i say this—

all crossings are hard
whether creeks, mountains
or into other lives

and we must always believe
in the snakes at our feet
just out of our vision

and we must practice believing
we *will* come through

—Martha Courtot

The mountain-moving day is coming
I say so yet others doubt it
Only awhile the mountain sleeps
In the past all mountains moved in fire
Yet you may not believe it
O man this alone believe
All sleeping women now awake and move
All sleeping women now awake and move.

The mountain-moving day is coming
I say so yet others doubt it
Only awhile the mountain sleeps
In the past all mountains moved in fire
Yet you may not believe it
O man this alone believe
All sleeping women now awake and move
All sleeping women now awake and move
All sleeping women now awake and move.

—Yosano Akiko[28]

God's Birthdance[29]

Once there was a God

who really didn't know she was a God.

In fact, she really didn't know
much about herself at all . . .
        she was asleep.

She mostly floated around on dark water
occasionally sinking down into its depths
or rising to the top like cream.

And it was dark . . .
        so dark.

I mean like nothing to look at,
just so much "not yet" floating around.

No one knows why . . . or how.
Maybe a wave startled him.
Maybe why and how are the wrong questions.
I mean, before God woke up
there was no why or how.

But at the moment God woke up,
Light shot out in all directions
and he caught himself smiling.

Then after a while he wanted to know what was beyond
the boundaries of his light, but he couldn't see,
being dark, so he said to hell with it, called it
Night, and resolved always to keep it separate.

And with this
God's creation began a march.

Day/Night Day/Night Day/Night Day/Night Day/
   Night

As God marched around his sphere of light
he thought that it would be better if he could
push all that water outside.
God wasn't sure why he found himself doing that,
he just felt that it made sense.
He left some of the water inside
but he collected it all together
and called it Seas.

God also wanted to name his sphere of light,
so he called it Firmament . . .
a fine vessel which floated
through the waters of its origin.
And everything was so neat and orderly.
Day and Night were neatly divided
and water and dry land were clearly separated
and God grinned broadly.

So God tried his hand at making something new
So he said to himself,

"I'll cause green life to appear on the dry land
and creature life to come from the Seas."

And God was proud because it made so much sense
and was so orderly.
So he called forth green life and he was so happy
because it just burst forth all over the dry land.

But even as he was smiling
a very strange thing happened.

Instead of the march,
green life started a waltz:

Plant/seed/new plant   Plant/seed/new plant   Plant/seed/
        new plant
This confused God
Instead of being in step with his Day/Night March
(led by Sun and fellow officers to keep Night in step)
green life waltzes.

It wasn't that he didn't like the waltz,
something deep inside him really did,
he was just confused.

Confused as he was, though,
he decided to stick to the The Plan.

So next he called forth creature life
hoping it would follow his March,
but secretly wanting it to waltz.

As he called,
creature life exploded out of the seas
and God found himself again smiling

as the waltz intensified
as it danced
and swirled
out of the ocean
into the air

up onto the land
and joined in
with green life's waltz.

Creature/seed/new creature   Life/after/its kind   Tree/
    fruit/new tree

And God tapped his foot to the waltz
all the time
wondering
why it was happening, and
why he was enjoying it.

I mean,
all that dancing and partying going on
didn't exactly fit in with the Orderly March he had intended

He knew the answer went deep . . .
as deep as the oceans of his birth.
So he thought to make a mirror of himself
in order to see his image:

I'll make a person like myself
then maybe I'll know why
I want to march and waltz at the same time.

So God very carefully made a mirror,
making sure not to leave anything out.

At last it was done.

And God turned and peered into the mirror.

At first he rubbed his eyes to make sure they were focusing
Then he laughed outright at the joke he had been
playing on himself.

For the mirror showed not one
but two images: a he and a she marching and waltzing

like sides of the same coin
linked together like two sides of the same coin.

So God understood
and they joined in the birthdance.

—David Wilson

5.
Articles, Lectures, Reflections

This chapter includes materials used in the workshop and related materials gathered from participants after the workshop ended. They are included not only to complete the record of what went on and for reflection on the workshop in retrospect, but also to demonstrate the depth and power of analysis that the women's movement has evoked in all of us—scholar, student, professional, amateur. Women have been working hard at setting the record straight, retrieving their own history, speaking out about their own experience. Women have also begun to examine the contradictions between the old consciousness and the new consciousness that have been created by their asserting their right to name their experience themselves. The work in this chapter testifies to the seriousness of the feminist challenge to accepted traditions in the fields of theology and anthropology. It points toward resolution of some of the contradictions between the old and new consciousnesses.

The chapter ends with two personal statements reflecting on the experience of the workshop. These attest to the power of reclaiming one's own voice to call out to God and are therefore a fitting close to the handbook.

The Politics of Liturgical Change

Linda Clark

In a remark which prefaced an address on liberation movements in the Third World, John Bennett said, "The church not only perpetuates the oppression of women in our culture, it causes it!"[1] Bennett did not explicate his statement that day; yet those of us acquainted with the Judeo-Christian tradition and its theology could indulge in quite a lengthy discussion of this topic. Two interrelated aspects of the movement to liberate women provide perspectives for the work of changing the language of the liturgy. The first is the notion that by incorporating female images of God and women's experience into the language of prayer, sermon, and liturgy we work to overcome the devaluation of women in this culture. The second is the notion that working against the devaluation of women in this way we also work against the devalued notion of human sexuality in our culture, since women are carriers of the symbol of nature and sexuality. The remainder of this essay will deal with suggestions and strategies for the process of liturgical change in a church setting.

In *Beyond God the Father*, Mary Daly makes the observation that as long as God is male, males are gods.[2] Now there are several ways to unravel the meaning of that statement. But the one that is the most germane to our interests is linguistic. It goes without saying that using male language for God means that somewhere in the far reaches of our psyches God becomes male.[3] Yet how exactly does that work? What is the relationship between the language of the culture and its social order? Another way to approach this problem is to ask the question "Why is there such a stir when words—little puffs of air with hisses and clicks in them—say one thing and not another? Why not simply use female words for God?" The answers to the last set of questions are found in the answers to the first set: One cannot begin substituting female words for male words in the liturgy willy-nilly, because language is not an arbitrary thing, changed at will. Language derives its meaning from the social structure of the culture which uses it: Changes in language imply shifts in the commonsense view of human experience in a particular cultural milieu.

Our idea of what belongs to the realm of reality is given for us in the language that we use. The concepts we have settle for us the form of the experience we have of the world. It may be worth reminding ourselves of the truism that when we speak of the world we are speaking of what we in fact mean by the expression "the world": there is no way of getting outside the concepts in terms of which we think of the world. . . . The world *is* for us what is presented through those concepts. That is not to say that our concepts may not change; but when they do, that means that our concept of the world has changed too.[4]

The battle being waged over the language of the liturgy is really a battle of world views between those who wish to come to terms with the male dominance of the culture and those who do not.

A more detailed look at the way language works will help to illumine both the problems we face trying to incorporate female images of God into the language of the liturgy and the *necessity* for it. Let us take the sentence "God is a father." It is a metaphor which uses the more commonly known entity "father" to describe aspects of the nature of God. "Father" is the thing we know something concrete about: Therefore we attach all those meanings to the subject of the sentence. We apply the connotations of the word father to God. We can see this process working in many metaphors: "The Lord is my shepherd / I shall not want" and "God is King above all gods." We know about shepherds and kings, their qualities and our social relationships to them, and we therefore know something more about God when we apply these terms to God. However, not only does the association of father with God say something significant about God, it says something significant about fathers too.

As the philosopher Max Black points out in an essay about metaphors, there is an interaction between the two terms in a metaphor: Therefore the qualification of meaning applies from fathers to God and from God to fathers.[5] There is a change of meaning taking place in both directions across that little word is: God is fatherlike and fathers are godlike. That long association of God and father in our language has served to create and to reinforce the dominance of the patriarchal figure in our culture. It becomes next to impossible to imagine God in other terms in the face of the continued reiteration of the Father-image of God.

Our language provides us with only male words for God—the reality is that God is male.

It is the hope that, among other things, through the explicit association of female images with God, the source of ultimate value, the female in the culture will be extended a greater value, the implication being that women too have godlike qualities. The outcry against that very idea demonstrates the importance of language changes. How can a woman, a second-class citizen, a sex object, have attributes that are godlike?

Conversely, women who work against their own devaluation in the culture recognize the importance of changes in the language, because those changes imply their own revaluation of themselves and can also cause such a revaluation. The words themselves are a means of consciousness-raising which force people to reconsider the origins of their reactions to such a change.

Let us now turn to a consideration of the phrase "God is a mother." This metaphor works in similar ways to the one with father in it. An interaction is set up between the two words which works to elucidate the meaning of the phrase. However, there is one important difference between the two phrases which has nothing to do with the fact of their being metaphors or with the particular words used. It is that the "father" metaphor is the older of the two and therefore carries less of the specific coloration of the words. The "mother" metaphor is new to us and therefore carries the particular connotations of the culture not mediated by more abstract and general usage. That the connotations of the word mother carry an implicit devaluation is almost impossible to escape under those circumstances.

"But," as one woman exclaimed in a discussion of this point, "this may result in the devaluing of God rather than the valuing of women!" Such a change emphatically signals a theological shift, but it may not be in a totally negative direction. The association of God with mother brings the deity down into our midst. Indeed, the very "motherness" accomplishes the process of making God more concrete. Mothers are in charge of the everyday, ordinary, and highly concrete business of living. They provide basic survival in concrete terms—food, clothing, and shelter. They handle it, with their hands, although according to the dominant myth about the "average" American family, fathers provide the money for it. The association of the ordinary business of living with God through the metaphor of "mother" will surely change the image of God. It undermines the notion of God as Total Otherness. Thus this change does not have to result in devaluation; it may extend to God an approachability that we have been loath to assume in the past.

Another important implication for our society of the use of female imagery for God lies in the resulting association of sexuality and God, since one of the most vivid cultural symbols that women carry is that of the sexual being. One of the greatest sources of the oppression of women derives from the association of female sexuality with sin. Here the church and the Christian tradition should stand condemned as the source and sustainer of women's oppression. Often the reaction against the use of female imagery for God derives from the incapacity to associate the ultimate source of value with the polluter of "man-kind."[6] It stems from men's projection of their own negative attitudes toward their sexuality onto women, who then become the source of temptation and the cause of their lust. To begin to use female images for God throws into confusion the network of ambivalent attitudes and sexual hostility against women.

To think that the liberation of women will come about through changes in language alone is naive. Women and men must work to change the "face of power" in the church so that the situation in which the words "God is a mother" are spoken reflects equality among the sexes. It is important to understand that the relationship of power or recognized social authority between the people who speak words and those to whom words are spoken influences the meaning that each sentence carries.[7] The sentence "God is a mother" spoken by a male seminary professor and heard by a group of laypeople will be interpreted in a different way than if those words were addressed to them by a woman in their own midst. In each situation the sentences are the same. Yet those who speak them exist at much different levels of recognized authority in the church. How that sentence is heard and the discussion which follows in response to it shifts according to the relationship of power among the people.

Despite the complexity of the issue, the language of the liturgy must be changed. As each wave of resistance arises it must be faced and worked through. The language excludes the female from the idea of God and explicitly includes the male, which works to reinforce the male dominance of the culture and the devaluation of anything associated with the female. Most of the biblical narrative is told from the point of view of men; most ministers are men. This obvious one-sidedness is masked through use of universal terms which imply that what the male sees, everyone sees. We are only beginning to explore the wide divergence in the experience of men and women hidden behind the usage generalized from male experience alone.

What follows is an exposition of ways to undertake changes in the language of liturgy. It is a beginning—suggestive rather than authoritative—since each situation will differ. Changing the language of the collective expression of belief of a group of people is really a process of consciousness-raising and mutual exploration. It involves changing people's ideas about reality—which suggests changing their ideas about God and about themselves. This is my particular list; blank pages follow for you to add your own. In consciousness-raising the content of the enterprise is heavily dependent on the experience and imagination of those undertaking it.

My first recommendation is to *find your own support group* among your parishioners. What you are about to begin is a long and arduous journey—one that a single individual cannot undertake with expectation of much success. You need the wisdom and support of many people. Collective action has a momentum that will carry you over the rough spots. Support groups are also valuable sources of criticism and fresh ideas.

The initial task of this newly formed group is to work to *understand the resistance to changes in language* about God by uncovering its own resistances to it. This type of self-analysis and mutual criticism helps to avoid the development of an "us/them" attitude which plagues many such ventures in which the change of language about God is used as a weapon to overcome the opposition and render it powerless. If one meets the resistance in people with the knowledge that we are really all in this business of change together (which in reality we are—the lure of complete annihilation of one's opposition is compelling but unrealistic!), the possibilities of real change are greater. However, this is much easier said than done.

When you begin, start with the easiest and least threatening thing: changes in prayers and sermons in reference to human beings rather than to God. Leave the Trinity and the Lord's Prayer for later. *Celebrate the smallest victories:* the slightest changes and the conversion of the least defensive person in your congregation. *Take the long view.* To think that you will accomplish the complete transformation of the liturgy in a year is to agree implicitly with the critics who say that the issue is trivial.

Work on many levels. When you once realize that you are working to change ideas about the nature of God and the commonsense view of human experience, then you can see that there are many subsidiary paths to follow to the main goal. Putting women in positions of recognized authority in the church is one; starting study groups on women in the Bible is another. Pointing to those obscure and behind-the-scenes places women have done wonders in the church accomplishes the basic purpose of valuing women's experience. Not only do we want women in positions of recognized authority in the church, we also want to honor the billion or so hours women have stitched and baked the church into solvency and the ghetto kids into summer camp. Those women's organizations in the church that have been the brunt of many jokes—often by feminists—should finally get the recognition that they deserve.

The *educational program in the church* is an immensely valuable resource in this process of liturgical change. As is so effectively demonstrated in Phyllis Trible's lecture (see page 104), there are many female images of God in the Bible that are obscured by the sexist gloss which covers it. Too, scholars are rewriting the history of the church to include the women that are invisible and have been deleted. Groups of women meet to tell the story of their own religious lives. Groups creating nonsexist resources for worship add to the growing list of published materials. So much of this "church" business needs demystification. The ordinary parishioner views most of public religious life as the property of the professional, the trained clergy. Any attempt to give laypeople the tools to express their own religious convictions helps to pave the way for the broadening and transformation necessary for people freely to adopt alternative, less male-dominated images of God.

And finally, *choose your battles carefully*. There are some you will never win, people and groups that you will never convince. A healthy respect for your own limitations will lengthen the days that you remain at the barricades, to extend the military metaphor.

The foregoing is a beginning, a sample of things to do. The work that we do to incorporate female images into talk about God is important for the church and for ourselves. Worship that is free of sexist language and that incorporates women's experience can be a powerful source of healing and strength that will sustain us—women and men—in the work for justice in the wider community.

Ways to Change the Language of Liturgy

Ways to Change the Language of Liturgy

The Process: Promises and Pitfalls[8]

Meganne Root

"The personal is political." This early tenet of the women's movement invited each woman to look inward and to find in her own experience the effects of her oppression as a woman and her hope and motivation for change. Feminists considered sexism to be a deceptively benevolent form of injustice. While in some circumstances women were the victims of dramatic and overt cruelty—more of this violence against women is reaching public notice in recent times—they were most often debased by events that took place quietly, every day, behind closed doors, in their private lives by forces they could not see or name. These same women were encouraged by feminists not to trivialize the quiet inequities they had endured. They were to speak out and view their own understanding of these inequities as authoritative. They were to create a political solution to what before had seemed to be personal problems.

One such political solution was the development of nonhierarchical forms of interaction in groups, using as a model the consciousness-raising group. Women's groups stuggling to embody this ideal of personal and political integrity faced many questions. If hierarchy is to be avoided and each person is to be her own authority, what need is there for leadership? What form does leadership take? Should women work toward a common analysis, with common goals and strategies? How are these discussions influenced by the model of leadership used in them? Should women work on consensus models? Should we strive to enable each person to express herself freely, to receive the respect if not agreement of others, and to feel herself supported and validated whatever her views?

The women's movement has neither abandoned its original ideals nor resolved the difficult issues they raise. The promises and pitfalls of an educational process that attempts to be true to feminist goals of shared leadership was certainly alive among us at Grailville as we addressed ourselves to the task of discovering meaningful images for feminist Christian worship.

The planners were interested not in worship abstractly conceived but in worship as a vehicle for people to draw closer to the liberating and spiritual dimensions of life, to God and to Jesus Christ, as some would say. The Christian perspective invited us to a process that was analogous to the feminist one: "Let us be true to our deepest selves. There we will find the key to our anger and to our hope." New images of our sources of strength were needed if worship was to be a means to this end. And conversely, new images would themselves emerge naturally if a genuine spirituality, in an atmosphere free of male domination, could be experienced and shared.

A description of the process may be in order here. A carefully arranged series of activities was scheduled by a planning group well in advance. After an initial hello, a meal, a brief worship service, and a short overview of the week, each participant chose a photograph from a large display and received the full attention of the group as she showed the picture and spoke about herself. This experience of self-disclosure and affirmation was followed by several sessions where we approached our spiritual depths through the imagination, through sounds and music creating visual and verbal images, and through body movement and the exploration of space. Interspersed among these activities, guided discussions of the nature of worship and a lecture on female images of God in the Bible took place. Only then, halfway through the week, did we start to design our own rituals and to plan for a more ambitious worship service as a culmination to the week. And only then did we go more deeply into the issue of the meaning of the Eucharist for Christian feminists and the problems of liturgical change in a church setting.

Regular worship activities were also planned in advance. These included a traditional Roman Catholic Lauds said and sung every morning, a silent ritual meal, a series of guided meditations, and a rite based on the story of Demeter and Persephone. This last rite incorporated materials from advocates of post-Christian feminist spirituality. Lauds was explicitly and traditionally Christian. The contents of the other worship events varied across a wide range of cultures.

Leaders and resource people had different skills and different roles within the group. Some gave information, some focused discussions, some helped people identify and express their feelings, some shared specific talents in the arts, meditation, and liturgical design. Many played several of these roles. Each in her own particular discipline or field of interest contributed to the week's collective task of designing new worship experiences.

A core of resource people had developed the basic schedule and had agreed upon the underlying educational and theological assumptions of the workshop prior to the week. However, many decisions were made during the week by the planning team: in daily "Breakfast Sessions," during several evaluation meetings, and during open planning meetings. Participants took part informally in many of these sessions. They also shared in decision-making indirectly by taking part in small groups that met three times during the week. These groups had leaders who functioned in a loosely defined moderator role. The "shape" and task of the groups was left up to the participants. During these meetings people had time to express confusion, disappointment, insight, excitement. They could develop a more intimate group in which to make suggestions and test out new ideas. The moderator brought relevant information from her group to the members of the planning team, giving them the "pulse" of the whole group and some idea about how to modify the existing schedule.

In sum, the planners chose a process in which a certain amount of structure and background information was provided by resource people. This skeleton functioned to point the group away from established concepts and norms and toward their own experience as a source for images of God and new forms of worship. The participants used these activities to explore their own creative processes and to affirm the fact that their own deep inner experience of the holy was the true basis for new theologies, new rituals, and new or transformed worship forms. The structure, the way in which the resource people functioned within it, and the body of background information were predetermined. The various theological perspectives, the images based on them, and the forms in which they were ritualized were the creation of the particular group that gathered there.

Would that I could say that the above process proved to be the solution to problems of leadership and modes of education true to feminist principles! Would that I could report that every-one quieted down, meditated, prayed, walked, talked, thought, sang, painted, ate, slept, and partied, found God, poured out her heart in perfect and revitalized forms of Christian worship replete with female images of God, and refreshed and renewed packed her bags and returned home! We did all those things in some form or another. Much was accomplished of real integrity, much of it was spiritually profound. Yet throughout there was an undercurrent of conflict and dissent that indicated the knot-tiness of the problem of process and change. What happened?

The week was largely a success: much of what the planners and resource people had hoped would happen did happen. The women who gathered there appreciated the time out from their work and study routines, from their persistent efforts to create change in resistant institutions. They especially enjoyed being in a supportive group of women of diverse ages, backgrounds, and religious traditions. They found many elements of the week spir-itually enriching and were stimulated and affirmed by the wide variety of approaches to worship. Some felt that the obvious ten-sions between feminism and Christianity had been faced in a significant and liberating way. The materials shared by resource people and developed by participants were impressive and valuable.

Several times during the week, however, a number of partic-ipants questioned aspects of the educational process. They found it too authoritarian and not true to the feminist and Christian values being espoused by various resource people. These critics for the most part affirmed the value of scholarly presentations but found other leadership styles inhibiting. Was the authority of each person, resource person and participant, being recog-nized and validated? If so, shouldn't participants be taking full responsibility for the process, perhaps teaching more skills to one another, devoting more time to group discussions without a cho-sen leader or without a preceding, preplanned talk? Should par-ticipants themselves have planned the week's activities together in order to respond to the most immediate needs and interests of the group? Another opinion voiced contradicted the above, asking more for materials that could be tried out and adapted to particular situations rather than exercises designed to produce the materials. It became clear in the midst of such discussions that there was a lack of trust in the group in the process and in the style of leadership chosen by the planners. The question of leadership remained an unresolved one. Amid the rhetoric, some of it contradictory, genuine feelings were being expressed about the nature of authority and its inhibiting qualities in educational circumstances.

Here is a summary of the observations about the issue of leadership as it emerged in the group.

1. There was no consensus as to what qualifies persons to assume leadership roles.

2. While many women were critical of the validity of degrees issued by male-dominated institutions, the women with more traditional academic training and rank were most easily accepted as authorities by the group.

3. It was harder to accept leadership from those among the planners whose experience was with marginal institutions or whose educational expertise derived from a solid experiential rather than an academic base.

4. It was harder to accept direction from someone who was not very different from the participants themselves.

5. If someone assumed a leadership role based largely on personal power, she had to have that power legitimized in some way by the group itself.

6. Formality of presentation was attacked; informality of presentation was attacked; lack of presentation was attacked.

There are several possible explanations for this form of interaction among a group of women:

1. It is highly improbable that in a group the size and diversity of this one one would find total conformity to any structure.

2. Women are unused to having power; they use it tentatively, which is unnerving in a group.

3. Women are so accustomed to experiencing the exercise of authority and power as oppressive that they generalize this oppressiveness to include any situation in which authority is present.

4. Working with one's imagination and one's ideas about God

produces fears of self-revelation and vulnerability. Defensive behavior is normal in such situations, and often it is projected on to "safer" and less personal issues, such as leadership style.

All or none of the above may be true; I include the list simply to indicate that the issues of power and authority are far more complex than the rhetoric would have us believe. We are suspicious of traditional structures of authority, so we rely on personal ones. Yet we do not understand the dynamics of power well enough to handle them effectively.

This experience reminds us once again that women still have few opportunities to be recognized as leaders and to share freely their skills and resources. We learned several lessons about planning from the conflict generated among the women gathered at Grailville:

1. The educational process and its rationale should have been more clearly stated on the initial flyer, at the opening session, and throughout the week.

2. More detailed correspondence with the participants prior to the program would have been useful, using a questionnaire to give the planners more specific information about the participants, to help them tailor the work of the week more closely to their stated needs.

3. The women could have been more strongly encouraged to bring materials from home (music, prayers, poetry, theological investigations) to share with one another.

4. The phrase "mutual resourcing," which appeared on the flyer, was more rhetoric than reality. Finding ways to do that more effectively would have enriched the experience for many.

There, in sum, are some of the pitfalls. The promise is embodied in this book and in the changes that many of us went through during that week and since then in small ways in our own lives. The promise of this particular experience in feminist education is well summarized by one woman who wrote: "I have spent so much time before trying to get affirmation from without, from others. I found affirmation coming from within myself. Instead of actually 'receiving' something, I have more a sense of participating in a process—open-ended—which has generated a process of my own which is also open-ended."

A Sermon: Wrestling with Jacob's Angel[9]

Linda Clark

I would like to talk to you about words, a particular set of words, words about God. Words about God do not control all that we know about God; indeed, words do not control all that we know, period. Layers of human experience defy the processes of language, as any artist will tell you. But for us Protestants, whose forefathers threw ritual, idol, and art out of the church and elevated the Bible and its verbal interpretation to the center of their religious assemblies, words about God are of supreme importance—and even that is an understatement.

The words we have to use in the biblical narrative and in worship are sexist; that is, they and the images that they evoke exclude the female from the deity (not the feminine, the female) and obscure the fact, through the continual reference to God as "he," that the image of God is both male and female. Words we use here put women in their place—either directly as in 1 Timothy—"Let a woman learn in silence with all submissiveness. I permit no woman to teach or to have authority over men; she is to keep silent. For Adam was formed first, then Eve; and Adam was not deceived, but the woman was deceived and became a transgressor. Yet woman will be saved through bearing children, if she continues in faith and love and holiness, with modesty" (RSV)—or indirectly by never referring to them, assuming that experience at center stage is the same as experience on the periphery, assuming that relationship to God is the same for both men and women: a male—a man, son, and father—relating to a God which is called Man, Son, Father, and a female—a woman, daughter and mother—relating to a God which is called Man, Son, Father.

And words are not mere accidents, something made up on the spot out of nothing. The exclusion of "she" to refer to God is not just an oversight, a linguistic mistake, a quirk to be easily remedied through reediting.

The importance of words about God was brought home to me in a very dramatic way this summer at a seminar on Meso-

American mythology. There in the foothills of California just above the Napa Valley I came in contact with a religion that was androgynous. The religion of the Mayan and Aztec civilizations included male and female gods, and often the gods were simultaneously male and female. Indeed, one of the highest aspects of the deity in the Aztec religion is *Ometeotl*, from *ome*, meaning two, and *teotl*, meaning God. The Aztecs believed that "the origin of the world and all human beings was *one single principle* with a dual nature (male and female). [This dual god] conceived the universe, sustain[ed] it and creat[ed] life."[10] Yet despite this duality, the god is always spoken of in the singular grammatical form. There is a plural form, but instead the Aztecs chose to refer to *Ometeotl* by the genderless (but personal) third-person singular pronoun. Since our language has no *personal* pronoun that is equivalent (our only alternative is "it," which is genderless but impersonal), there is simply no way to translate the Aztec concept of a personal androgynous God into English,[11] and no way for us to speak of a singular, personal androgynous God either.

The power of the androgynous quality of this religion took days to sink in, but when it did—when the study of the myths and figures of the Nahua-speaking peoples became something more than an intellectual exercise, when I was able to overcome the prejudice against these so-called "primitive" or "pagan" gods with which we Americans have been able to dismiss the religion of millions of people not white and western European— I stepped into a new land with a huge rush of emotion.

This entrance took place in conjunction with the telling of the myth of the Scabby God. In the story, the Scabby God is called on to create the fifth world—a job that the other gods reject because it involves the sacrifice of self-immolation. Now in the course of this telling, the seminar leader had alluded briefly to the fact that the Scabby God was androgynous, but because we have no pronouns in English that include both he-ness and she-ness, he had continually used the pronoun "he" to refer to the Scabby God. And I sat there, listening to this myth, a little bored, a little uneasy because I knew that when it came right down to it I wouldn't be able to sacrifice everything either, that I wouldn't be the Scabby God, that I was like the other gods in the story, filled with failings, cowardice, pride. As in all stories with heroes in them, here and in the Bible too, I found myself identifying with the followers, the hangers-on, the people on the periphery.

That night when we gathered in the seminar room, a slide projector was hauled out, and there projected onto a screen in all his hideous glory was the Scabby God, covered with scabs and sores—and he had breasts! And for some reason, seeing those breasts hanging there made that myth come alive for me. I hadn't been able to understand why the Scabby God would sacrifice *himself*—there I immediately identified the Other in the myth, the not-hero, the gods on the periphery, but I understood perfectly well why and how the Scabby God would sacrifice *herself*. And that's when I stepped into the new land: I was furious at that seminar leader and all the seminar leaders before him, both male and female, that for innumerable reasons had obscured the female aspect of God.

The next morning we all talked about it—both men and women—about what it had meant for us to realize that the Scabby God was at once both male and female, and we spent the rest of the seminar working together on this experience.

Then I returned to New York City, Union Seminary, and the God of Abraham, Isaac, and Jacob.

And I began to read, and found that if one would only look at the dirt swept under the rug of the church, in the corners and between the boards, in the things repressed, the gods ignored, those things persecuted and abused, dismissed as trivial, the scholars not read or accused of bias or sloppy methodology—in short, the debris of the established hierarchy of the church, both ecclesiastical and academic, there was a lot of information about the female aspect of deity, about women and their notion of God. And I asked myself, "Just who is the God of Sarah, Rebekah, Rachel, and Leah?" Is she different from the God of Abraham, Isaac, and Jacob? Is that a trivial question? Is it irrelevant? Is the fact that I would entertain the notion that it is both trivial and irrelevant the result of the misogynist attitudes nourished by the church all these centuries?

With that question I would like to approach the problem of the words of the Bible from a different but related viewpoint by telling the story of Jacob wrestling with the angel as I have experienced it—the process of the incorporation of Jacob's story into my story. This is one of my favorite passages in the Old Testament. The first time I "found" it (or it "found" me) was during a particularly dark period in my life. My sister-in-law, who had also been my best friend in college, had developed cancer, and during a two-year period while she was dying I moved in with her and my brother and their three children, coping simultaneously with instant motherhood, the grief of her death process, and the difficulties raised in such a tightly knit family by anxiety, anger, bitterness, and fear. I was alternately a rock and a wreck, patching up and holding together my family, being patched up and held together by several friends and colleagues. And through it all I held on to that picture of Jacob alone struggling with God.

What struck me about that story at that time was that Jacob was wounded wrestling with God and in the process all the names that had worked before left him and he was given a new one. That was what was happening to me. I felt terribly wounded, and all the neat categories that had ordered my existence to that point dissolved, and I was faced with chaos. I was in desperate need of new names, and although I longed to do it, I couldn't take a few weeks off, flee to some place of retreat to confront what I was going through and discover the new order, and be given the new name. I had to come up with the new names then and there, in the midst of getting the boys off to school, working at Union Seminary, visiting Peggy in the hospital, trying to find ways of talking about illness to a six-year-old, doing the dishes, shopping for school clothes, picking up at birthday parties, talking endlessly to everyone, exhausted. . . . And I needed the new names not only for the people around me but also for myself—I needed the names—because I was anxious, frightened, bitter, and angry, badly wounded and limping.

During work with another myth last summer, I was reminded of the story of Jacob and went back to it to read it again, to find it again, and the first thing I saw when I picked it up this time was the bit about sending the women across the river: "The same night [Jacob] arose and took his two wives, his two maids, and his eleven children, and crossed the ford of the Jabbok. He took

them and sent them across the stream, and likewise everything
that he had. And Jacob was left alone . . . [Genesis 32:22ff, RSV]"
Those lines jumped out at me. "Why hadn't I seen them
before?" I asked. What *power* Jacob had to be able to rid himself
of all that—all his possessions—and be alone to wrestle with
God! What were the women doing on the other side of the river?
The way the story is told, it makes it sound like he dismissed
them in order to wrestle with God. Did he consider all that secondary, trivial, in comparison to the real issue—that of wrestling
with God? What does it mean for women to read those words,
women who all their lives battle with feelings of being excluded,
secondary, trivial, struggling against external prejudice and
internal misgivings, always finding themselves on the other side
of the river? How oppressed we have been by the notion that
what we do, no matter what it is, *automatically* puts us on the
wrong side of the river: "Who me? I couldn't possibly have the
insight, the qualifications, the heart, the right to act or think the
way I do—another degree, a better job, a different mate—
another opinion, another child—and I will have confidence in
who I am, in what I do—always somewhere else, someone different—but never here, never this person, here on the wrong
side of the river among the women, the children, the slaves, the
cattle, the goats . . ."

Now, it is obvious what is different about my response in the
first experience with this story and my response in the second
experience. The first time, I identified with Jacob; the second
time, I identified with Rachel and Leah and the slave girls. And
although the first experience is closer to the meaning of the text
and its traditional interpretation, the second adds a dimension to
the text that is indispensable to me as a religious woman in this
culture. Why? Let me illustrate:

The most important point the text makes is that Jacob is alone
when he wrestles with God. What a powerful image that is!
Jacob rids himself of all his encumbrances, his relationships, his
possessions, everything he has worked so hard to get, everything
he loves—his wives, his status, his slaves, his children; he sends
across that river everything that spells out his old identity. And
gradually he loses his last defense—his cunning—as he wrestles
with that angel. He is totally vulnerable, naked, defenseless.

Jacob's old names he sends away in order to receive the new name, the blessing he cries out for, the name Israel.

And how I longed for the solitude of Jacob during those months living with my brother! How I wanted to send that whole mess across the river so I could at last grasp this thing, this nameless God, that I struggled with. But that was the one thing I never had; I never was alone. With a shock I realized that mothers of young children are rarely alone, and that was one of the hardest aspects of the whole ordeal—adjusting to the loss of solitude. And no matter how much I might desire it, the times of solitude were accidental almost—times when I found myself alone, the children in the park with a baby-sitter, my brother at work, the housekeeper with a friend. Then I would sit, resisting the impulse to clean, put away, wash, fold, and the myriad other tasks that housework mentality brings with it, and try to empty my mind and to confront this situation that I had found myself in. But it never worked out that way.

And yet in a time when solitude was a luxury I continually struggled with God. My vulnerability, my defenselessness, my dependence on God, my namelessness in the face of death were impressed on me—almost exclusively in the midst of other people—as a result of other people. The whole chaotic experience breathed the new name: for me in that situation, "alone" meant not solitude but being stripped of several illusions that I had harbored, finding myself totally vulnerable among my friends and family, not away from them, needing new names desperately and saying that to them, not away from them.

Where the new name came from resembled more closely Rachel's and Leah's side of the river than Jacob's—there among the women, children, slaves, and goats. I do not think that the text denies that—it's just that the images obscure it. All of us— men and women alike—are impeded in the process of crossing the river to Rachel and Leah if the story is always told from the point of view of Jacob. All of us—men and women alike—are impeded in the process of crossing that river to Rachel and Leah by the use of images and words that exclude women and their experience from serious consideration.

One last way of looking at the problem of words about God: If we are created in the image of God and we are both male and female, if God has no gender and transcends the sexual differences between us, why not simply alternate God the Father and God the Mother week by week in the Trinitarian formula? That suggestion raises enormous problems, not the least of which has to do with the image of the mother we have in this culture: "Mom," "The mother-in-law," "mother which rhymes with smother." There is a difference in meaning between the expressions "to father a child" and "to mother a child." And there is a difference in meaning in the quality of relationship between a father and a son and between a mother and a son. Perhaps the words of the Bible are right: The God of Abraham, Isaac, and Jacob is a Father God, and the only relationship we can have to him is that of a son to a father. Perhaps we delude ourselves into thinking that Yahweh is Mother to us and that we can relate to her as a daughter relates to a mother.

And when it all finally comes out, the questions seem to be "What is the relationship between words and the Word?" and "What is the relationship between images of God and the reality that they point to?" I only can ask these questions now, point to some of the problems and some of the ways to a solution. But I think that we are really trapped if we are consigned to the reality described by the words that we and other Christians and Jews before us have used to speak of the nature of God. God is at once Mother and Father, Daughter and Son, and transcends those distinctions too, and that is the image in which we are created. We all are Abraham and Sarah, Isaac and Rebekah, Jacob, Rachel, and Leah. And we must create new images, new stories, to speak of that reality.

The Gift of a Poem:
A Rhetorical Study of Jeremiah
31:15–22[12]

Phyllis Trible

Phyllis Trible's presentation constituted one of the highlights of the Grailville workshop. Using the image of a woman searching for a lost coin (Luke 15:8), she invited us, "while

acknowledging the dominance of male language in scripture,"
to light a lamp, sweep the house, and search diligently for what
has been lost—the image of God male and female in
scripture.[13]

She then directed our attention to a partial portrayal of male
and female that suggests the image of God in Jeremiah 31:15-
22. We present here that rhetorical study as an introduction to
the exciting and deeply moving feminist scholarship of Phyllis
Trible's book God and the Rhetoric of Sexuality.[14]

Jeremiah 31:15–22 is a drama of voices.[15] These voices organize
structure, fill content, and mold vision to create a new thing in
the land (cf. v. 22b), and this new thing is the poem. Its five
strophes form a chiasmus with the voice of Ephraim at their center (vv. 18–19). Surrounding this center are the voice of Rachel
(v. 15) and the voice of Yahweh (vv. 16–17), on the one side, the
voice of Yahweh (v. 20) and the voice of Jeremiah (vv. 21–22)
on the other. This encircling pattern mirrors the relationship
between female and male throughout the poem and thus provides a vision of both the parts and the whole.

The first strophe (v. 15) announces the weeping of a woman.
Centuries ago Rachel died while giving birth to the son of her
sorrow (Genesis 35:16–20), and now from her grave this ances-
tral mother laments the subsequent death of all her children:

> A voice on a height![16]
> Lamentation can be heard,
> weeping most bitter.
> Rachel is weeping for her sons,
> refusing to be consoled for her sons:
> "Oh, not one here!"[17]

This structure shows a mother embracing her sons with tears
and with words. Her tears are profuse: lamentation; most bitter
weeping; Rachel weeping, refusing to consoled. By contrast, her
words are few: only two *(kî 'ēnennû)* before speech fades into
the silence of desolation. Yet this fading speech belongs to an
enduring voice. Directed to no one in particular, and hence to
all who may hear, the voice of Rachel travels across the land and

through the ages to permeate existence with a suffering that not even death can relieve (cf. Matthew 2:18).

More specifically, Rachel's voice carries into the next strophe (vv. 16–17). Its second word, voice *(qôl)*, repeats the first word of strophe one; likewise, the weeping *(mibbekî)* of this voice persists *(bᵉkî; mᵉbakkâ)*. Hence to Rachel, Yahweh now responds, using the feminine singular imperative:

> Keep your voice from weeping
> and your eyes from tears.[18]

Promise motivates and sustains this divine imperative. From a general assurance it moves to a specific pledge, with the formula "oracle of Yahweh" *(ne'um Yahweh)* intervening to reinforce the promise:[19]

> for *(kî)* there is a reward for your work—
> oracle of Yahweh—
> they shall return from the land of the enemy.

The next line repeats this pattern and posture:

> and there is a hope for your future—
> oracle of Yahweh—
> sons shall return to their borders.

In both instances, the verb return *(šûb)* marks God's pledge. Repetition stresses its importance.

As the opening imperative indicates, strophe two focuses upon Rachel. Speaking to console her, Yahweh never draws attention to the divine self. No first-person pronouns occur. Conversely, at least once in every line, possessive pronouns address Rachel: your voice, your eyes, your work, your future. To be sure, Rachel's consolation is to come through the return of her sons; yet they are mentioned with restraint. Yahweh first refers to the children only as "they" (v. 16), and in the parallel line (v. 17) where "they" becomes "sons" (this word providing another verbal link with the first strophe) God neither names these children nor attaches them to Rachel. In spite of translations,[20] the deity does not say "your sons." On the whole, the divine voice in this stanza emphasizes neither the deity nor the sons but rather the woman. She dominates.

But the third strophe changes emphasis (vv. 18–19). Concern for a mother leads to consideration of her children. The sons are named and they are quoted. Ephraim, at the center of the poem, is the center of attention. With verbal emphasis,[21] Yahweh introduces him: "Truly I have heard Ephraim rocking in grief." The verb hear (šāma') is a specific link between strophes one and three, but with differences. As the third word in strophe one, it is a passive voice, with no agent of hearing specified: the voice of Rachel can be heard on a height. As the first word(s) in strophe three, it is an active voice, with the I of Yahweh as subject and the son Ephraim as object. This object speaks remorse. Although Rachel's voice was so pervasive that it lacked a specific audience, the words of her children address God directly:

"You whipped me, and I took the whipping
  like an untrained calf;
bring me back that I may come back,
  for you are Yahweh my God.
For after I turned away, I repented;
  and after I came to my senses, I slapped my thigh.[22]
I was ashamed, and I was confounded.
  because I bore the disgrace of my youth."

Ephraim implores and confesses. Three times he uses the verb turn (šûb) in the double sense of physical movement and religious change. The last of these usages recalls his exile and apostasy: "after I turned away." The other two ask God to restore him to the land and to his deity: "bring me back that I may come back." Theologically, the repentance of Ephraim is an act of God; geographically, the return of Ephraim is the work of God. These two occurrences of the verb echo Yahweh's promise to Rachel in strophe two: "they shall return from the land of the enemy . . . sons shall return to their own country." Now strophe three accounts for that promise: Ephraim imploring God with a voice of repentance and confession.

Rachel cries; Yahweh consoles; Ephraim confesses. Thus the

poem has moved to its center. Words of a mother and words to a mother converge upon her child. Then, with variations in order and in content, this pattern recurs in the next two strophes so that female semantics encircle the voice of the son.

Strophe four is Yahweh's voice (v. 20). The *Revised Standard Version* translates it:

> "Is Ephraim my dear son?
> Is he my darling child?
> For as often as I speak against him,
> I do remember him still.
> Therefore my heart yearns for him;
> I will surely have mercy on him,"
>   says the Lord.

As in the preceding strophe, God speaks in the first-person singular and names Ephraim—a name occurring in approximately parallel places (vv. 18a, 20a). Thus verbal links continue between adjoining stanzas. At the same time, however, strophe four matches strophe two in position and in speaker. Together they surround the center. On the one side, Yahweh consoles; on the other, Yahweh contemplates. But these similarities involve dissimilarities. For instance, the first-person singular of the deity, as well as divine possessive pronouns, dominates the language of strophe four. Neither appeared in strophe two, where Rachel dominated. Consequently, attention belongs here to Yahweh (not to Rachel). Moreover, Ephraim is the object of this attention. God names him, as the deity failed to do in strophe two, and God claims him—for the first time ever. A threefold utterance of question, motivation, and conclusion probes the divine relationship to this child. Particles introduce each of the three sections.

An interrogative particle poses a rhetorical question: "Is Ephraim my dear son? my darling child?" Having heard Ephraim rocking in grief (v. 18), Yahweh now considers him. But the question is a moment of hesitation that combines distance and intimacy. If Ephraim is the darling child of Yahweh, it is that Ephraim who God has punished; it is also this Ephraim who is seeking restoration. In contemplating the child, Yahweh hesitates with a question that suggests but does not declare tenderness. Perhaps this deity shares a mother's suffering. After all, are not the children for whom Rachel weeps also the children of Yahweh?

The motivational clause, introduced by the particle *kî-middê* (as often as), moves toward a resolution; yet it elicits opposing interpretations.[23] Do its two cola contrast divine judgment and mercy?

> As often as I turn my back on him,
> I still remember him. (NEB; cf. JB)

Or are these cola a totally negative statement?[24]

> For since I spake against him,
> I do earnestly remember him still. (KJV; cf. RSV)

Or are the cola a full affirmation of love?

> That as oft as I mention his name
> I so longingly think of him still? (AB)

Context joins content to decide meaning. Preceding this line, Yahweh has already promised Rachel that children will return to their own land, and Ephraim has already repented. Following this line, Yahweh speaks of compassion for the children, and they are urged to return home. In other words, judgment has no power in the poem. This motivational clause proclaims love: "For the more I speak of him, the more I do remember him." To speak of the child is to remember him lovingly,[25] even as Rachel remembers him. Indeed, God's memory is hope for Rachel's future (cf. v. 17).

Finally, with striking imagery, the climactic line of strophe four confirms God's love for Ephraim. Here all distance is overcome. To introduce this line, the particle *'al-kēn* (therefore) points not to a logical progression of thought but rather to the energizing power of language.[26] Moving from anthropomorphic imagery in the rhetorical question of the first line to anthropopathic levels in the motivational clause of the second, Yahweh comes, in the conclusion of the third line, to the inner recesses of human existence where the physical and the psychic unite to convey the depths of divine love. Female imagery abounds. First, Yahweh utters words that the woman in the Song of Songs uses to describe erotic play:

> My beloved put his hand to the latch,
>   and my inner-parts trembled *(mē'ay hāmû)*
> within me. (5:4)

Reversing the order of these two words, Yahweh speaks of her inner parts trembling for Ephraim the child. In some other passages, inner-parts parallels womb (Genesis 25:23, Psalm 71:6, Isaiah 49:1; cf. Ruth 1:11). Hence, the first colon of this concluding line can be appropriately translated "therefore, my womb trembles for him."[27] Support for this translation comes in the second colon. Its two words, both verb forms, are metaphors for compassion, and the base of this metaphor is the term womb *(reḥem)*.[28] Thus an exclusively female image extends meaning here to a divine mode of being: "I will truly show motherly compassion upon him," says Yahweh. Furthermore, these two verb forms parallel the verb forms of the preceding line. Together they emphasize the tender memory and the earnest love of Yahweh for Ephraim: "I do remember him lovingly [v. 20b] ... I will truly show motherly compassion upon him [v. 20c]."[29]

To sum up, strophe four is the voice of Yahweh the mother. Parallels between Rachel and Yahweh occur in each of its three sections. The rhetorical question calling Ephraim a "darling child" suggests that God identifies with Rachel caring for her children. The motivational clause recalls Rachel remembering her lost sons with tenderness. And the conclusion makes explicit the maternal metaphor for God. As Rachel mourns the loss of the fruit of her womb, so Yahweh, from the divine womb, mourns the same child. Yet there is a difference. The human mother refuses consolation; the divine mother changes grief into grace. As a result, the poem has moved from the desolate lamentation of Rachel to the redemptive compassion of God.

Female imagery surrounds Ephraim; words of a mother embrace her son.[30] My translation is:

> Is Ephraim my dear son? my darling child?
> For the more I speak of him,
>   the more I do remember him.
> Therefore, my womb trembles for him;
> I will truly show motherly compassion upon him.
>
> Oracle of Yahweh.

Still there is more. Ephraim confesses; Yahweh contemplates; now Jeremiah commands. The message of God's compassion must be delivered to her child, and that is the role of the prophet. Hence, strophe five is the voice of Jeremiah.[31] Speaking to the child, his voice lacks the tenderness of Yahweh's, although it carries the divine words of restoration. Mood, but not message, changes. Furthermore, this strophe absorbs form, content, and meaning from throughout the poem; at the same time it is full of surprises. The finale is both summary and innovation. In the overall structure it corresponds to strophe one; yet it is longer— a sign of end-stress.[32] It also has a verbal link to the opening strophe, but with a different meaning. The nouns *tamrûrîm* appear at the end of the first line of both strophes.[33] In the former instance, the word means bitterness; in the latter, guide-posts. A poem beginning with a mother crying bitterly for her lost children concludes with a prophet commanding them to make guideposts for their return home. Despair has become hope. Moreover, along the way a new thing has happened to the children: they change sex. At first, male; at last, female. Ephraim the son becomes Israel the daughter. Jeremiah speaks to a woman. This change of imagery converges upon the center of the poem to surround male with female.

Jeremiah speaks with imperative and with impatience. After all, since restoration has been granted Israel, the nation ought to return immediately. Five feminine singular imperatives urge haste. Their form matches Yahweh's command to Rachel in strophe two: "Keep your voice from weeping" (v. 16). Similarly, feminine second-person pronouns also recall other language of this strophe:

> Set up waymarks for yourself;
>   make yourself guideposts.
> Consider well the highway,
>   the road by which you went.
> Return, O virgin Israel,
>   return to these your cities.

Of these five imperatives, two return to the verb *šûb*. Twice this verb appeared in strophe two as God's pledge to Rachel that her children would return. Twice this verb appeared in strophe three as Ephraim's request that he be returned. Now twice this verb appears in strophe five as Jeremiah's command that Israel return. What was promised and what was requested, God has made possible. To return to the land is to return to God. But the vocabulary of return had still another meaning in strophe three, the meaning of exile and apostasy. Ephraim said, "for after I turned away . . ." (v. 19). In a rhetorical question,[34] strophe five incorporates this meaning too: "How long will you dillydally, O turnabout *(haššôbēbâ)* daughter?"[35] Hence, between strophes three and five, three verbs respond to three verbs in sequence and in meaning.

Jeremiah's question of urgency leads to the final, climactic line of the poem:

> For *(kî)* Yahweh has created a new thing in the land:
>   female surrounds man.

Like the rest of strophe five, this line both absorbs and gives meaning to the entire poem. Its words move between repetition and innovation. At the very beginning of the poem stands the prophetic formula "thus says the Lord," so that even the voice of Rachel comes under its rubric.[36] This formula comes again at the opening of strophe two, which is indeed Yahweh's speech. Further, the two phrases "oracle of Yahweh" emphasize the point. In strophe three, Ephraim confesses faith with the words "for you are Yahweh my God." Strophe four, the voice of Yahweh, concludes with the formula "oracle of Yahweh." Thus the appearance of the Tetragrammaton in strophe five belongs to a constant pattern. The difference is that here Yahweh neither speaks directly nor is spoken to; rather, Yahweh is spoken about. The poet has taken over to announce God's new creation, and this new thing requires a new verb, *bārā'*—a verb used throughout the Old Testament only for the creative work of God.[37] Accordingly, verb and object match to proclaim the unique. Yet this new creation is "in the land," a word that echoes strophe two even as it reverses meaning. Yahweh who promised that "they will return from the land *('ereṣ)* of the enemy" (v. 16) now creates a new thing in the land *('ereṣ)* of their home. Altogether then, this declaration, both in form and in content, alternates between innovation and continuation.[38] A part mirrors the whole of strophe five.

Now the reversal of meaning for the term land recalls other reversals. For instance, the bitterness of Rachel has become guideposts for the return home. More important, the male Ephraim has become the female Israel. This switch in sexual identification anticipates the final colon where language is again out of order. Subject and object turn sexual patterns upside down: "female surrounds man."[39] The colon moves between mystery and meaning.[40] All its words are new; none of them has appeared elsewhere. They are what they say—a new thing in the land. But this new thing belongs in the poem and in the poem finds its meaning. Innovation and continuity interact. Accordingly, the two nouns of this proclamation—one female, the other male—belong to a series of images developed throughout the poem. Specific female images are Rachel weeping for Ephraim, Yahweh showing him motherly compassion and Israel replacing him. In the last line of the poem, the word female *(nᵉqēbâ)* resonates with all these images. As a generic term, it can include all females. Used in Genesis 1:27 to identify one human sex, this word occurs in poetic parallelism with the phrase "image of God"—a parallelism approximated in Jeremiah 31:22b. Furthermore, in the Genesis passage (and similarly in Jeremiah) this noun is an object of the verb create *(bārā')* with

God (in Jeremiah, Yahweh) as a subject. Thus its usages in Genesis are an external witness to the kind of internal function it has in Jeremiah. As an inclusive and concluding referent, female *(nᵉqēbâ)* can encompass poetically all the specific female images of the poem.

But to encompass is to surpass. The verb surround contributes to its subject, female, a power that moves beyond the other female images in the poem. Although it is present in the connotations of the verb itself,[41] this power becomes apparent through a word-play in the last two lines.[42] Calling Israel a turnabout *(haššôbēbâ,* v. 22a) daughter, the poet juxtaposes immediately the description of female surrounding *(tᵉsôbēb,* v. 22b) man. While two very different images of the female are associated here through assonance, this association yields a radical transformation with the positive image superseding the negative in Yahweh's new creation. Hence, the climactic affirmation that female surrounds man has power to move beyond the other female images of the poem even as it includes them. This affirmation can dry up the tears of Rachel; it can fulfill the compassion of Yahweh;[43] and it can overturn the apostasy of Israel. As an inclusive and concluding referent, it surpasses poetically all the specific female images of the poem.

The male images, on the other hand, are reinforced by the poem's last word, man *(geber).* In strophes one through four, the male vocabulary has terms designating youthfulness: son *(bēn)* in strophes one, two, and four; young man *(naʿar)* in strophe three; and child *(yeledh)* in strophe four. All these words refer to Ephraim. Parenthetically, the female words for Israel in strophe five also stress youth: virgin *(bᵉtûlâ)* and daughter *(bat).* Thus the nation, male or female, is portrayed throughout as young. Yet at the same time Ephraim suggests in strophe three (the center strophe) that he is a grown man with the disgrace of his youth behind him (v. 19). Now the term *geber* can absorb all these male meanings.[44] Outside witnesses include Job 3:3, where *geber* describes a baby boy; Proverbs 30:19, where it portrays a young man; and Exodus 12:37, where it specifies adult males. *Mutatis mutandis,* these meanings fit Ephraim so that the word *geber* develops further continuity in the male vocabulary of the poem. But it is also a new word that contributes new meaning: the nuance of virility. Perhaps the frequent application of *geber* to warriors or to heroes demonstrates best this persistent connotation.[45] The nuance itself, rather than its military applications, participates in our poetic context to enhance further the radical reversal that is the new thing of the poem. Thus it is the virile male, child to adult, who is surrounded by female. As both continuity and innovation, the term man *(geber)* completes the phrase "female surrounds." All together these three new words interact with images throughout the poem.

Having no one specific referent, then, the three new words of the final colon wander throughout a work of art both to receive and to give meanings. Accordingly, female surrounding man is Rachel the mother embracing her sons with tears and with speech; it is Yahweh consoling Rachel about Ephraim; it is Yahweh declaring motherly compassion for Ephraim; and it is the daughter Israel superseding the son Ephraim. And it is more than these images. Female surrounding man has power to dry up the tears of Rachel; to fulfill the compassion of Yahweh; and to overturn the apostasy of Israel. And it is other than all these images, for it is Yahweh's creation of a new thing in the land. In short, it is the poem:

> Words of a *woman:* Rachel cries (v. 15)
> Words to a *woman:* Yahweh consoles (vv. 16–17)
> Words of a *man:* Ephraim confesses (vv. 18–19)
> Words of a *woman:* Yahweh contemplates (v. 20)
> Words to a *woman:* Jeremiah commands (v. 21)

"Female surrounds man": this declaration is the denouement of an aesthetic object. The structure, content, and meaning it gives is the structure, content, and meaning it receives. In other words, the poem describes itself. Since it is an organic unit, an interlocking structure of words and motifs, it resists extrinsic formulation and requires imaginative interpretation.[46] To hear its language is to perceive its being.

Lo, then a new thing in the land: Yahweh creates a poem.

The Wanderings of the Goddess: Language and Myth in Western Culture[47]

Catherine A. Callaghan

"The Greeks did not believe that the gods created the universe. It was the other way about: the universe created the gods."[48] Although this statement by Edith Hamilton is an oversimplification, it underscores a universal principle. The divine realm must correspond to the political world below.[49] Changes in the social order may destroy this correspondence, in which case tension will be felt until the world above realigns itself. Language behaves much like the realm of myth in that both derive their significance from the social order rather than the other way around.

Many people, including some feminists, have made grave errors in reacting to the content of both language and myth without due regard to their source and historical development.[50] Usually they start their investigations too late, at a period when patriarchy was well established in Western culture. If we wish to understand the true correspondence between myth, language, and social order, we must trace them to their roots, which for our purposes lie in two areas: pre-Hellenic Greece and pre-biblical Mesopotamia.

Stage 1: The God and the Goddess

In Greece, the Neolithic Age lasted roughly from 6000 B.C. well into the third millennium B.C. Its economy was based on herds and small-scale agriculture supplemented by hunting expeditions. Under such circumstances, group survival was more dependent upon plant and animal fruitfulness, an observably feminine function, than either warfare or the hunt. Fertility idols were common in the form of female figures with large hips, typical of the Near Eastern mother-goddess cult.[51] Authorities dispute the number of languages spoken by these "Pelasgians" and their linguistic affiliations, agreeing only that they were non-Greek,[52] but one would expect several languages in a region composed of small, self-sufficient communities.

Agriculture may originally have been in the hands of women, as is often the case in primitive societies today. Memory of this early state of affairs persisted into the Bronze Age, which spread through Greece from Asia Minor, bringing with it the swing-plow, metal-working, the potter's wheel, urbanization, large-scale sea trade, and social stratification.[53] This culture reached a peak in the Minoan civilization of Crete with its luxurious palaces. Priestesses not goddesses were often dominant in the frescoes, and key rulers and temple heads may have been women.[54] Some communities lacked defensive walls, indicating a relatively peaceful period.[55] Male and female probably enjoyed more nearly equal power in both the mortal realm and the kingdom of the gods.[56] Consequently, I call this the stage of the God and the Goddess.

The earliest levels of Greek mythology reflect this period. Hesiod speaks of an autochthonous creatrix called Gaia (later Gē), whose name was a pre-Greek word meaning earth. She was doubtless known by different names in different localities.[57] One of these was Demeter the Corn Goddess, who not only controlled the seasons but actively participated in them. The barren season resulted from her grief over her daughter Persephone's departure for the underworld, and it lasted until Hades again released the maiden to the surface of the earth. Persephone's earlier name was Persephassa, and the -ssa suffix marks her as another pre-Hellenic deity.

Stage 2: The Rape of the Goddess

The invading Hellenes entered Greece sometime between 2100 B.C. and 1900 B.C. They were Greek-speaking Indo-Europeans with a different cultural orientation. Their original homeland is uncertain, but it may have been somewhere in eastern Europe.[58] Since they left no written records, our knowledge of their culture derives from words that can be reconstructed from cognates in the daughter languages. These include a large number of kinship terms, and an examination of them plus evidence from Roman, Homeric, and early Scandinavian law codes shows that their culture was probably patrilocal, patrilineal, and patriarchal.[59]

Their chief deity was °dyews pətēr "Father Zeus," originally a sky god.[60] There was probably a prior emphasis on the male activity of warfare. They found the means of turning warfare into territorial expansion during the third millennium B.C. when they acquired the horse.[61]

Tales of the centaurs may reflect the movement of mounted archers into areas where the horse was unknown.[62] The slow conquest of Greece by the Hellenes had a profound effect on the social order. The warrior rather than the farmer became primarily responsible for cultural survival, and he would be male because men are usually stronger than women.

The female fertility images disappeared and were replaced by hilltop sanctuaries.[63] Whether or not the Greeks won a particular engagement, a victorious chieftain would find it increasingly inappropriate to worship a fertility goddess. Tension was felt between the divine realm, which mirrored a more peaceful era, and the world of hard, contemporary reality.

The Pax Minoica on Crete ended during the fifteenth century B.C., probably through a combination of earthquake, revolt, and an invasion from the mainland.[64] Afterward, the Mycenaean Greeks assumed power and their language became dominant. The decipherment of the Linear B tablets shows that men ruled from then on.[65] Later frescoes depict chariot scenes and warriors,[66] and a crucial tablet reveals that a pantheon of Greek gods, including Poseidon (Neptune), Hermes (Mercury), Zeus, and Hera, had already been established.[67]

Hesiod appropriately gives Crete as the birthplace of Zeus, grandson of Gaia and the first deity in the genealogy with a certain Indo-European etymology. Stories of battles between Zeus and the Titans could represent uprisings of the indigenous inhabitants against the Greeks.[68]

More to the point, the numerous affairs of Zeus with local goddesses, which I call "The Rape of the Goddess," might correspond to the male seizure of local temples. The great oracle of Delphi was possibly under the patronage of an earth goddess until Apollo slew the guardian dragon and assumed control himself.[69]

The Corfu pediment of about 600 B.C. shows that Medusa, the female monster slain by Perseus, was originally a Great Goddess.[70] Goddess figures either relinquished their power voluntarily or were slain. The three-hundred-year courtship of Hera by

Zeus might have represented the time necessary for the vast synthesis between the old and new religions.

Such transfer of power is not unique to Greece. In primitive societies, the shaman is usually chosen as the result of a personal calling, which in some groups can come to either a man or a woman. As the society grows more complex, religious ritual becomes stylized and its ecstatic element (direct contact with the divine) is diminished. Power is often transferred to a predominantly or totally male priesthood. The old religion, or an ecstatic variant of the new state religion, may survive among fringe groups, usually led by women or low-status men.[71]

In time, the bureaucratic Mycenaean civilization degenerated into the fair-and-square plunder of the Heroic Age and finally into the chaos of the Dark Ages (1200 B.C.–800 B.C.). Rule reverted to tribal chieftains until the emergence of the Greek city-states in the eighth century B.C. The latter were often ruled by a *tyrannos* who had seized power through a military coup d'etat. Sculptors specialized in idealized nude male figures.

The flowering of the intellect in fifth-century-B.C. Athens ("the Cradle of Democracy") was for male citizens only. Medicine became professionalized under Hippocrates, thereby shrinking the functions of any local midwives or healers. As professions and positions of power passed from women, so did reasons for giving them an advanced education. At that point, the great poetess ceased to appear.[72]

Once women received only a rudimentary education, everyday experience would seem to confirm the idea that they are in all ways inferior to men. Even Plato, who thought that the best should rule and that the best might occasionally be a woman, agreed that the average woman was inferior to the average man in every respect.[73]

When Aristotle asserted that it was inappropriate for a poet or playwright to make a female character clever, he was in part reflecting the fact that the wise woman did not play any role in Greek society.[74] Athenian women of the fourth to second centuries B.C. were expected to be silent, subservient, and secluded. They took part in making wills, some family councils, and their own sororities, but in little else, and they usually married men much older than themselves.[75]

119

To recapitulate, I have tried to link the decline of women in Greek history to social circumstances rather than to male pride or envy, as is the custom in some feminist circles.[76] Frequent warfare made the soldier more important than annual fertility. The growth of cities with their storage facilities further lessened the dependency on yearly bumper crops and made a police force necessary. Rulers would naturally be chosen from the military or need military training, and eventually it would seem "natural" to exclude women from all positions of importance.

I have also shown how conceptions of the divine realm change to correspond to the world below, although there is often a time lag.[77] Even under Zeus, the Olympian goddesses still shared rulership with the gods for a time, but power soon shifted to the latter. Hera became subservient to her husband, and Athena declared herself to be "all for her father." The virtues of the perfect Athenian woman were epitomized by the Hearth Goddess Hestia, who meekly yielded her position on Olympus to the god Dionysus.[78]

Stage 3: The Death of the Goddess

The status of women in Near Eastern civilizations went through a corresponding decline while Greece was still in the Neolithic Age. Sumeria, located in what is now northern Iraq, is the earliest known civilization, dating from the fifth millennium B.C. until 1750 B.C.[79] It also provided us with our oldest decipherable written records.

Early Sumerian woman had important legal rights. She could hold property, engage in business, and qualify as a witness.[80] Polyandry may also have been practiced.[81] Otherwise, the society was already strongly patriarchal.

Sumerian goddesses likewise played a key role in the origin myth. The autochthonous creator was the Sea Goddess Nammu, perhaps reflecting the dependence of arid Sumeria on irrigation from the Tigris and Euphrates rivers. Both the God Enki and the goddess Nimmah were instrumental in the creation of human beings.[82]

During the third millennium B.C., the area was overrun first by the Akkadians then by the Babylonians. Their mythology had a strong misogynist element. The creator Tiamant, also a Sea

Goddess, was overthrown and slain by her descendant, the war god Marduk, in one of the goriest scenes in literature.[83] Marduk then became permanent ruler of the pantheon.

As in pre-Hellenistic Greece, the greatest women lived in the early period. There was one female physician and one great poetess (Enheduanna, a high priestess to the Moon God).

By the time of the Babylonian law codes (2050 B.C. to 1700 B.C.) marriage was strictly monogamous and women were regarded as the property of their fathers or husbands, although they could themselves hold property. The only professions mentioned for women were tavern-keeper, priestess, and prostitute.[84]

Here also political and geographical factors played a decisive role. The whole area was subject to flood, famine, and scorching heat. Fertility depended upon the maintenance of a huge irrigation system, and there was a constant threat of invasion. Masculine strength was prized, and weaker woman was tolerated because she bore children.

Abram (later Abraham) came from Ur of the Chaldees (another Babylonian city), probably in the early part of the second millennium B.C. when the Hellenes were expanding through Greece. The status of Babylonian women and goddesses had by then reached an all-time low, and Abraham's descendants succeeded in killing the Goddess altogether.

Unlike Zeus, Jehovah was technically nonsexual,[85] but he was always designated by the Hebrew pronoun *he* and described largely in terms of male imagery that reflected the realities of patridominant Hebrew life. The few exceptions usually compared him to a woman with a child.[86] Goddess worship was not merely eclipsed, but forbidden on pain of death. Likewise, there was no room for the priestess or any other female religious functionary. Nor did the Bible allocate any special rights to women as women, although of course they had certain rights as human beings.[87]

No celestial marriage was possible once the Goddess was eliminated. Worship lost its earthiness when the priest and priestess did not mate, at least symbolically, and the allegory of love was translated onto the spiritual plane.[88]

Judaism (and, later, Christianity) was divorced from the natural cycle to a degree hitherto unknown. God gave Adam and

Eve dominion over the earth with no general injunctions to revere natural forces, although a form of stewardship was implied in some biblical passages. Therefore they were largely free to manipulate nature without fear of supernatural consequences. This worldview greatly facilitated the controlled experimentation that centuries later would lead to the rise of science and technology.

Judeo-Christianity was also linear. Celebrations formally marked events that occurred only once, like the Passover or Easter, rather than the ever-recurring seasons. The Angel of Death passed over the Jews once, and Christ died and was resurrected a single time, while Persephone came above ground every year. The Bible introduced a concept of history in which both the cosmos and the individual had a definite beginning, passed through a series of nonrepeatable stages, and would some day come to an end or arrive at a permanent state.

As we saw previously, linearity had also gained a footing in late pagan Greek cosmology. Zeus became the third and permanent king of heaven. Festivals commemorating his marriage to Hera were held annually in many Greek cities. The Pythian games celebrated Apollo's victory over the monster Python (or Delphyna). By the early centuries A.D., the intellectual concept of Zeus had become almost as abstract and all-embracing as that of Jehovah.[89] These factors facilitated the spread of Christianity through the Western world.

Stage 4: The Splintering of the Goddess

The Bible says that each person is made in the image of God. Such a doctrine stirs analogical associations that work more powerfully than any syllogism. If the sole deity is male, even symbolically, then the "genuine" part of a human being is considered masculine. In other words, the concept "man generic" comes to mean "man male."

What then happens to woman? It has been frequently observed that our culture treats her largely in terms of her relationship to man. The symbolic level goes even further. She is reinterpreted as the higher and lower aspects of man (both male and generic). This tendency is evident even in the New Testament. In Paul's much quoted Ephesians 5, woman is treated metaphorically as the lower part of man[90]:

"Wives, submit yourselves unto your own husbands, as unto the Lord. For the husband is the head of the wife, even as Christ is the head of the church. . . . So ought men to love their wives as their own bodies. He that loveth his wife loveth himself."[91]

1 Peter 3 also urges wives to be subject to their husbands, adding "If any [husbands] obey not the word, they also may without the word be won by the conversation of the wives." This passage anticipates the notion of woman as redeemer of fallen man, so aptly embodied in Augustine's mother Monica and of course the Virgin Mary.

We see that the idea of woman as the inspirer of man is at least two thousand years old. It did not develop from the tradition of courtly love a thousand years later, as some feminists have implied.[92] Instead, I believe that courtly love became a possibility because of a prior tendency to idealize the good woman.

It has become fashionable to ascribe the misogyny of Christian writers to a projection of male sexual guilt onto women. While the charge is partially accurate, it does not account for the fact that condemnation and praise of women so frequently went hand in hand. Saint Bernard of Clairvaux in the eleventh century A.D. saw every woman as a threat to his chastity but was devoted to the Virgin Mary.[93]

Misogyny reached a peak in the *Malleus Maleficarum*, issued in 1487 by Pope Innocent VIII, which became the manual of both Catholic and Protestant witch-hunters for the next three hundred years. Comments included: "All wickedness is but little to the wickedness of a woman. . . . What else is woman but a foe to friendship, an unescapable punishment, a necessary evil, a natural temptation."[94]

Yet this diatribe was immediately followed by the statement "But for the good women there is so much praise that we read that they have brought beatitude to men and have saved nations, lands, and cities."[95] Moreover, one of its authors, James Sprenger, enrolled thousands in the Confraternity of the Holy Rosary.

A full-time inspirer is still a full-time servant, and the classical image of the Virgin Mary as Queen of Heaven has been used by conservative Catholics and Orthodox Christians as an argument against any further concessions to women's rights. As a result, some feminists have considered Mary's influence totally negative.[96] But they would do well to study what happened in Germany when Martin Luther extirpated this last remnant of the Goddess. By closing the nunneries, he deprived women of their chance for an advanced education. For the next two hundred years, female German intellectuals were mostly Catholic or Jewish.[97]

We have seen that woman lost her self-identity with the Death of the Goddess and the subsequent decline of her influence in society. From then on, her self-image was formed by men (the phenomenon of the Blank Mirror). Woman still retained some positive identity in Judaism as bride and mother, but even that was diminished with the asceticism of Christianity.[98] As the concept "man generic" fused with "man male," woman was splintered into its higher and lower aspects.

This fusion accounts for the fact that quest figures in literature are nearly always men.[99] Everyman is male, although Wisdom and Good Deeds (the higher aspects of himself) are female. The knight in search of the Holy Grail and Faust are both male, although the savior figure for the latter (Gretchen) is again a woman. In *Paradise Lost*, Eve can be regarded as a symbol for the lower part of Adam, which led him into sin. But by repenting first, she also led him back to God.

We do not know any of the pre-Greek words for "man generic," "man male," and "woman," since their writing systems have not yet been deciphered. But the Proto-Indo-European words for these concepts have been reconstructed as follows[100]:

1. Man generic
   a. $PIE°\widehat{gh}_bmōn$ "earthling," related to words meaning "earth."
   b. $PIE°mon$-, possibly related to °manu- "hand" or °men- "to think."
   c. $PIE°mr̥-t$- "mortal," from °mer- "to die."
2. Man male
   a. $PIE°wĭr$-, probably related to °wēys "vital force."

Attested Forms in Early Indo-European Languages

Language	Man generic	Man male	Woman
Classical Latin	homō < °ĝh₆mōn-	vir < °wĭr-	fēmina °dhēmnā
Oscan	humuns (pl.) < °ĝh₆mōn-	ner "man of rank" (also Umbrian) < °ner-	
Umbrian	homonus < °ĝh₆mōn-	uiro (acc. pl.) < °wĭr-	
Classical Greek	anthrṓpos	anḗr	gunḗ
Gothic	manna < °mon-	waír < °wĭr- guma < °ĝh₆mōn-	qino < °gʷenā-
Old Church Slavonic	člověkŭ	mǫži < °mon-	žena < °gʷenā-
Sanskrit	manu- < °manu- puruṣa-	nar-, nara- < °ner- vīra- < °wĭr- pumaṅs-	nārī (fem. of nar-) jani- < °gʷeni- strī-
Avestan		nar- < °ner- vīra- < °wĭr-	jani- < °gʷeni- gɘnā- < °gʷ(e)nā strī-
Old Persian	martiya- < °mr̥t-	martiya- < °mr̥t-	

b. *PIE°ner-*, probably from words meaning strength, capability.
3. Woman
   a. *PIE°gʷenā, °gʷeni-*. Some scholars have related these forms to *° ĝen-* "to bear, beget," but such a connection is now considered unlikely.
   b. *PIE°dhēmnā-* "she who suckles," from *°dhēy-* "to suck."

To the extent that we can reconstruct them, Proto-Indo-European words for the three concepts were based on different roots.[101] Man generic (as opposed to the gods) was an earthling, a tool-user, and a mortal. Man male (as opposed to woman) was physically strong. Woman (as opposed to man) could suckle.

Reflexes of these roots still expressed the appropriate concepts in Classical Latin, Oscan, Umbrian, and Sanskrit (except for *nārī* "woman" from *nar* "man"). The situation in Classical Greek is unclear. *Anthrōpos* "person" may derive from a compound of *anēr* "man male," plus *ōps* "face" (i.e., "man-faced"), but the etymology is much in dispute. The Gothic reflex of Proto-Indo-European *°gh̯u̯mōn* "human" had already come to mean "man male" by the fourth century A.D.

As Christianity spread through Europe and patriarchy was intensified, the above semantic shift took place on a massive scale. In Vulgar Latin, the use of *homō* "person" was extended to include "man male" at the expense of *vir*, which eventually died out. This coalescence persisted in the daughter languages, as in Spanish *hombre* "man" (male and generic). The Germanic reflexes of Proto-Indo-European *°mon-* "person" underwent a similar shift to "man male." A derivative form came to mean "person" in all Germanic languages except English (i.e., German *Mensch*).

Christian missionaries may have been in the Slavic area from the fifth century onward, but none of the Slavic dialects was written down until the ninth century A.D. By that time Old Church Slavonic *mąži* (also from *°mon-*) had already shifted from "person" to "man male," and a new word *člověkŭ*, had been introduced for "person." Corresponding developments took place in all the other Slavic dialects. Serbo-Croatian went through the cycle twice as *čovjek* "person" expanded its range to include "man male."[102]

Words for "person" and "male" were usually distinct in Avestan, the sacred language of the Zoroastrians. But they coincided later in patriarchal Old Persia, where Darius the Great swore by the one true Avestan God, Ahura Mazda, and *martiya-* "person" came also to mean "man male." This shift continued under Allah as New Persian *mard* was restricted to the second meaning.[103]

European words for "woman" have undergone shifts in meaning consistent with the Splintering of the Goddess; that is to say, they tend to become either elevated or debased. Old English *cwēn* and *cwene* both originally meant "woman," but *cwēn* came to mean "queen" while *cwene* degenerated to "quean, harlot." German *Frauenzimmer* was at one time a room for the women at court, then it became a colloquial term for women, and it now has a derogatory connotation. On the other hand, Polish *kobieta* was at first an insulting term for a woman, but it has now become an expression of endearment.

We have seen that semantic changes often paralleled the conceptual changes attendant upon the Rape and Death of the Goddess, although these semantic shifts have traditionally been regarded as universal tendencies.[104] Evidence that they are culture specific comes from the matrist Iroquois. According to Holmer, Mohawk *ōkweh* "person, Indian" expanded its range to mean either "person" or "woman." The Seneca form *ūkweh* went one step further and now usually means "woman" in a respectful sense.[105]

Iroquoian women held the cultivated land, and clan membership was reckoned through the female line. Head women selected male chieftains and could depose them if they proved unsatisfactory. Women as well as men were religious functionaries, and Iroquoian cosmology featured a woman who fell from the sky.[106]

We can conclude that the socio-political sphere of a culture is the independent variable upon which the conceptual realms of myth, interpretive theology, religious observance, and language depend.[107] Changes in the latter spheres lag behind social change, a fact which sometimes helps us to uncover prehistory.

At the same time, we have shed light on one of the most vexing problems in linguistics: to what extent does language determine the worldview of a culture?[108] It would seem that both language and myth serve to sustain an ongoing worldview but cannot by themselves instigate change.[109]

Stage 5: The Resurrection of the Goddess

The extent to which the Goddess died in the minds of common people is uncertain. Throughout much of Catholic Europe, the Virgin Mary was regarded as the Mother Goddess, to whom one might take intimate problems, including those of fertility. But schooling and church authority constantly counteracted this conception and divested Mary of any independent powers. Yet the continual desire to deify Mary points to an imbalance felt by both men and women over an all-male God.

The ancient pantheon of gods was easy to project onto the whole natural and social order. In particular, the union of God and the Goddess was analogous to the human family, natural fruitfulness, and the mystical union of the higher and lower self. The Catholic Trinity allowed no such projection.[110] The following schema summarizes the viewpoint of many Catholics although the Trinity is considered to be ultimately a mystery.

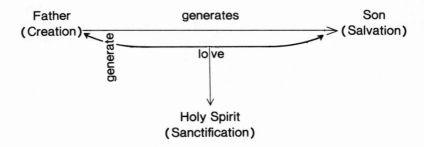

From early times, theologians have been aware of a symbolic imbalance, and some have tried to compensate by emphasizing the feminine attributes of the Holy Spirit. Vladimir Soloviev, a late-nineteenth-century Russian mystic, went so far as to postulate Sophia as a Fourth Hypostasis of God. Such speculation might provide a feminine symbol for male mystics, but neither

Sophia nor the sex of the Holy Spirit could alter the strange image of generation by a father and son.[111]

Today, we are faced with another hard fact of social reality— the earth is finite and we are filling it up. Unbounded technological exploitation is no longer possible. We have had some painful lessons in how mightily the Earth Goddess can retaliate when her domain has been abused. Linear progress must be modified by a new respect for natural cycles, hopefully into an upward progressing spiral.

In addition, physical strength has become less and less important for cultural survival. It is being replaced by the equally sinister vector of the high I.Q.[112] Once again women are on a more nearly equal footing with men.

How should women respond to the situation? First, by placing an image based on achievement in the currently Blank Mirror. This phase must precede attempts to reform either the divine realm or language. Moreover, any suggested reforms must be along lines that can be accepted by the culture at large.

There can be no doubt that the double usage of "man" serves to sustain the notion that "human" means "male," but I do not believe in forcing the substitution of "person." I have noticed that television stations tend to reserve "chairperson" and "spokesperson" for women. A preliminary study by one of my students based on a sample of thirty subjects showed that half listed "female" as their first impression of the sex of "chairperson of the committee." Thirty percent gave "male" and only 15 percent answered "either sex" (one failed to respond). Likewise, over half thought that "Ms. Adams" was an unmarried women's-libber.[113]

All the follow-up studies showed that "chairperson" was failing as a sex-indefinite referent. In one study, 37 percent gave "female" and another 37 percent gave "male."[114] In a third study, 47 percent stated "female" and 37 percent said "either sex" (all subjects were high school students).[115] A fourth study, restricted to students at Ohio State University where the use of "chairperson" has been mandated, showed that three-quarters of them considered a chairperson to be "male," simply reflecting the ongoing social situation.[116] All three of these studies also confirmed the fact that "Ms." is becoming a substitute for "Miss."

Because of the energy behind the women's movement, the word "woman" is becoming charged with a dynamism it never possessed before. Why not press for "chairwoman of the committee" under appropriate circumstances? The sex-indefinite case could be covered by "chair."

"Co" and other proposed substitutes for the sex-indefinite pronoun are doomed to failure. To use them, people would have to speak English like a foreign language. Furthermore, they are unnecessary; we already have a perfectly good sex-indefinite pronoun, "they," which has survived two hundred years of persecution by male grammarians. Its use is again spreading to formal papers, and "he or she" could always be reserved for superformal situations.

The divine realm is again under stress. The image of an autocratic male God can no longer stir the majority of people, over half of whom are women in an individualistic, self-assertive society. New pagan religions have arisen that again worship the God and the Goddess and project their functions onto the natural sphere. There is hope some of them will survive as alternate faiths, partly through their affinity with the ecology movement.

Most people would prefer to work within the framework of conventional religions, but the traditional images continue to be a block. Catholics can symbolically reevaluate the role of Mary and emphasize strong female saints such as Joan of Arc. But a problem arises in that there is no way to incorporate Mary into the Godhead, and the symbolic consequences of her human state were felt in Pope Paul's recent decision against the priesthood for women.[117]

The most fruitful possibilities lie in a symbolic reinterpretation of the Godhead itself. Mary Baker Eddy proposed a century ago that "God the Father" be replaced by "Father-Mother God." Christians could call the First Person of the Trinity "Father-Mother" (or "Mother-Father"), thereby producing a much more vital image of creativity.[118]

But none of these proposals will yield fruit without long, hard work in the socio-political sphere by women themselves. Only when women achieve a set of relevant self-created images can there be a resurrection of the Goddess.

Reflection[119]

Phyllis Kuestner

I came carrying my suitcase to the quiet of the corner room in Benedicite, silently rolling the music of that blessing in my Quaker ears. Benedicite. Benedicite. I am the paradoxical stranger searching, always searching for home, knowing on some very basic level that I am already and always home. The sense of being "at home" is one of the most striking aspects of a stay at Grailville: that one may be oneself, free to leave pretense at the door as readily as one leaves shoes by the entrance of the Oratory.

The Chinese ceremonial meal was an important part of the week for me. It was part of the invention of ourselves as a group with shared meanings: a gift; the cup that runneth over and the empty chalice, elaboration, and simplicity. The whole experience contrasted sharply with the outer world of hurried meals, when all too often life is snatched from meaning in the rush to gulp it all down on the way to Somewhere.

The sense of being a woman on a quest is in itself cause for celebration. Grailville is a place where the quest is the focus. "No more second-hand religion," one woman said that first day. And there was a glorious assent from the group. "Image-breaking/Image-building" was organized on the basis of a fundamental confidence in woman's strength to live on into answers rather than needing a fail/sale schedule with predetermined answers given by exalted experts.

One of the reasons I attended the Grail session was that it fit in well with research I was doing on women and mysticism. The special resource speakers spoke with relevance to my research topic, but beyond that, the other participants spoke to my condition as a woman who worships. At Grailville I talked to women who experienced religion from various perspectives that differed greatly from mine.

Now after several months the old images begin to crack like ice in spring. I meet myself anew: a kind of conservative heretic. Still feeling "all beclothed with the love of God," I am full of thanksgiving, but echoing "No more second-hand religion."

| *Notes*

Chapter 1: Introduction

1. Rosemary Ruether, "Christianity and Feminism: Can a Male Savior Help Women?" *Occasional Papers*, United Methodist Board of Higher Education and Ministry, vol. 1, no. 13 (December 1976).

2. For a detailed discussion of this theory of the imagination, see R. G. Collingwood, *The Principles of Art* (London: Oxford University Press, 1958).

Chapter 2: A Working Definition of Worship

1. James White, *New Forms of Worship* (Nashville: Abingdon Press, 1971), p. 40.

Chapter 3: Exercises: Image-breaking/Image-building

1. "The Politics of Liturgical Change" (pages 83-89) is relevant here.

2. See "A Woman's Ritual" (pages 51-55) for an example of such a feminist worship experience.

3. See Rosa Shand Turner, "The Increasingly Visible Female and the Need for Generic Terms," *The Christian Century*, March 16, 1977, pp. 248-52.

4. Phyllis Trible, *God and the Rhetoric of Sexuality* (Philadelphia: Fortress Press, 1978), p. 202.

5. The litanies, prayers, and confessions included in chapter 4 of this handbook (pages 60-69) are products of a writing workshop.

6. Leonel L. Mitchell, *The Meaning of Ritual* (New York: Paulist Press, 1977), p. x.

7. Margaret Mead, "Celebration: A Human Need," *The Catechist*, May 1976, p. 54.

Chapter 4: Resources

1. From Arlene Swidler, ed., *Sistercelebrations* (Philadelphia: Fortress Press, 1974), used by permission.

2. Ibid., pp. 39-40. Used by permission.

3. From the song "Never Touch a Singing Bird." Words and music by Malvina Reynolds. © Copyright 1972 Schroder Music Co. (ASCAP). Used by permission. All rights reserved.

4. From *New Wine* (Los Angeles: Southern California-Arizona Conference of the United Methodist Church, 1969).

5. This style of meal was introduced at Grailville by Theresita Lee Wang, originally of Hong Kong, now living in Cincinnati, Ohio.

6. Mary Lee George-G, "Women Welcome the Equinox," *Womanspirit*, Vol. 4, No. 15, Spring Equinox, 9978 (1978), 6–7. Adapted by permission.

7. A longer version of the myth of Demeter found in Edith Hamilton's *Mythology* (Boston: Little, Brown & Co., 1942), pp. 57–63, may be substituted to good advantage if there is sufficient time to include it in the service.

8. "Thaw" by Martha Courtot. Used by permission.

9. "Benediction" (p. 85) in *Women and Worship* by Sharon Neufer Emswiler and Thomas Neufer Emswiler. Copyright © 1974 by Sharon Neufer Emswiler and Thomas Neufer Emswiler. Used by permission of Harper & Row, Publishers, Inc.

10. Trina Paulus, *Hope for the Flowers* (New York: Paulist Press, 1972).

11. "A Litany" by Sharon Owens. Used by permission.

12. "To the Goddess" by Catherine A. Callaghan. Used by permission.

13. Prayer by Estelle Petitt. Used by permission.

14. Prayer by Margaret Purdy. Used by permission.

15. Prayer by Phyllis Kuestner. Used by permission.

16. Poem by Bernice Smith. Used by permission.

17. Published by the Coalition on Women and Religion, Seattle, Washington. Used by permission of the Rev. Marie M. Fortune.

18. From *Woman-Soul Flowing: Words for Personal and Communal Reflection*. Reprinted with permission of the Ecumenical Women's Center, 1653 West School Street, Chicago, IL 60657.

19. Written for a worship service during "Theological Perspectives on Women and Violence," a program of Women United in Theologizing and Action, held at Grailville, June 1978. Used by permission.

20. "Wisdom Herself Speaks" by Estelle Petitt and Catharine A. Callaghan. Used by permission of the authors.

21. From *In Search of Eros* by Elizabeth Brewster. © 1974 by Clarke, Irwin & Company Limited. Used by permission.

22. From *In God's Image: Toward Wholeness for Women and Men*, ed. LaVonne Althouse and Lois K. Snook, p. 13. Copyright © 1976 Division for Mission in North America, Lutheran Church in America. Reprinted with permission.

23. Translated from the Latin by Jill Raitt.

24. From *A Daily Office* (New York: Mother Thunder Mission). Used by permission.

25. From *Revolutionary Patience* by Dorothy Sollee, trans. Rita and Robert Kimber (Maryknoll, NY: Orbis Books, 1977), pp. 51–52. Used by permission of Orbis Books and Lutterworth Press (England).

26. Adapted from the RSV by Marian Ronan.

27. From Martha Courtot, *Tribe* (San Francisco: Pearlchild, 1977). Used by permission.

28. From *Mountain Moving Day: An Anthology of Women's Poetry*, ed. Elaine Gill (Trumansburg, NY: Crossing Press, 1973).

29. Published in *Anima*, 3, no. 1 (Fall Equinox 1976), pp. 68ff. Reprinted with permission.

Chapter 5: Articles, Lectures, Reflections

1. Given on Alumni Day 1977 at Union Theological Seminary, New York City.

2. Mary Daly, *Beyond God the Father* (Boston: Beacon Press, 1973), p. 13.

3. Casey Miller and Kate Swift, "Women and the Language of Religion," *The Christian Century*, April 14, 1976, p. 353.

4. Peter Winch, *The Idea of a Social Science* (London: Routledge & Kegan Paul, 1958), p. 15.

5. See Paul Ricoeur, "The Language of Faith," in *Union Seminary Quarterly Review*, Spring 1973, for a succinct presentation of this idea.

6. Max Black, *Models and Metaphors* (Ithaca, NY: Cornell University Press, 1962). See chapter 3.

7. Dwayne Huebner, "An Educator's Perspective on Language About God," an address delivered at the Consultation on Language About God, Louisville Presbyterian Theological Seminary, October 3–4, 1977.

8. "The Process: Promises and Pitfalls" by Meganne Root. Used by permission.

9. "Wrestling with Jacob's Angel" by Linda Clark. Reprinted from *Union Seminary Quarterly Review*, vol. 33, no. 1 (Fall 1977). Used by permission.

10. Mary Ritchie Key, *Male/Female Language* (Metuchen, NJ: Scarecrow Press, 1974), pp. 20–21, quoted in Casey Miller and Kate Swift, "Women and the Language of Religion," *The Christian Century*, April 14, 1976, p. 353.

11. Ibid.

12. First published in the *Andover Newton Quarterly* 17 (1976/77), 271–80. Reprinted by permission.

13. Cf. Phyllis Trible, *God and the Rhetoric of Sexuality* (Philadelphia: Fortress Press, 1978), p. 200.

14. Ibid.

15. Not all scholars recognize Jeremiah 31:15–22 as a poetic unit. For instance, though allowing for a discernible pattern in vv. 15–20, Brevard S. Childs calls this section "a series of separate units loosely joined together"; vv. 21–22 are not included (*Memory and Tradition in Israel* [Naperville, IL; Alec R. Allenson, 1962], p. 40); see also Guy P. Couturier, "Jeremiah," *Jerome Biblical Commentary* 1 (Englewood Cliffs, NJ: Prentice-Hall, 1968), p. 326. On the other hand, John Bright sees vv. 15–22 as a poetic unit (*Jeremiah*, Anchor Bible [New York: Doubleday, 1965] pp. 275–76, 284–86); see also Muilenburg, "Jeremiah, the Prophet," *Interpreter's Dictionary of the Bible*, E-J (Nashville: Abingdon Press, 1962), p. 834.

16. For this reading rather than the traditional "in Ramah" see Matitiahu Tsevat, "Studies in the Book of Samuel," *Hebrew Union College Annual*, 33 (1962), 107–9; also Herbert Brichto, "Kin, Cult, Land, and Afterlife—A Biblical Complex," *Hebrew Union College Annual*, 44 (1973), 38–39.

17. At several places, including these two tricola, my translation of this poem is indebted to Prof. William L. Holladay. Following his suggestion, I understand the introductory word of this last colon as an emphatic *kî* preceding words of lamentation; cf. Jeremiah 4:8; 6:26. Cf. William L. Holladay, *A Concise Hebrew and Aramaic Lexicon of the Old Testament* (Grand Rapids, MI: Eerdmans, 1971), p. 155; see also James Muilenburg, "The Linguistic and Rhetorical Usages of the Particle *kî* in the Old Testament," *Hebrew Union College Annual*, 32 (1961), 135–60.

18. The word order in Hebrew is chiastic, with the imperative at the center: "from weeping your voice keep and your eyes from tears."

19. The two occurrences of the phrase "oracle of Yahweh" have been a problem for translators and interpreters as far back as the LXX, which omits both phrases as well as the entire beginning of v. 17; it also has a different reading for the ending of v. 17 (LXX, Jeremiah 38:16b–17). Cf. JB, NEB. My approach is to respect and interpret the final form of the Hebrew text.

20. E.g., KJV, RSV, AB, JB, NEB, NAB.

21. The infinite absolute *šāmôaʿ* precedes the finite form *šāmaʿti*, "I have heard"; see Ronald J. Williams, *Hebrew Syntax* (Toronto: University of Toronto Press, 1976), pp. 37–38 (sec. 205).

22. I owe this translation to Prof. Bernhard W. Anderson, who in a privately circulated essay has also studied this poem from a rhetorical perspective ("'The Lord Has Created Something New': A Stylistic Study of Jer. 31:15–22"). The last two lines of the quotation are from the RSV.

23. Differences in interpretation hinge on the meaning of the preposition *bᵉ* in the first colon and of the verb *zākar* (remember) in the second. The preposition may have either a positive or a negative value. Similarly, memory may be for weal or for woe; cf. Psalms 25:6–7; 74:22, 79:8; Jeremiah 31:24.

24. When translators choose a negative meaning for the first colon, it is not always certain whether they intend a negative or a positive meaning for the second, as, e.g., KJV.

25. Like the verb hear in v. 18, the verb remember here is an emphatic statement with the infinitive absolute preceding the finite form.

26. See Johannes Pedersen, *Israel* (London: Oxford University Press, 1959), vol. 1 pp. 116–23.

27. A translation arrived at in discussion with Professor Holladay. Cf. KJV: "Therefore my bowels are troubled for him."

28. See P. Trible, "God, Nature of, in the OT," *Interpreter's Dictionary of the Bible*, Supplementary Volume (Nashville: Abingdon Press, 1976), p. 368; on metaphor itself, see Philip Wheelwright, *Metaphor and Reality* (Bloomington: Indiana University Press, 1962).

29. Thus three of the four first-person speeches of Yahweh are syntactically the same (vv. 18a, 20b, 20c); see notes 19 and 23, above.

30. While I am interested in recovering female imagery for God, I am not interested in stereotyping either females or God; nor do I wish to stereotype love. Thus, one must not infer from anything written here that the love of God is a "feminine" attribute (as contrasted, e.g., with justice or wrath as a "masculine" attribute), or that motherhood per se is a loving mode of existence (cf. the two harlots in 1 Kings 3:16–28), or that the vocabulary of love in the Old Testament is exclusively female (even womb imagery encompasses paternal love; Psalm 103:13). Nor must one infer anything else that smacks of stereotyping. To the contrary, recovery of female semantics for God enlarges, deepens, and liberates our understanding of the biblical God, human creatures, and, in this particular instance, love.

31. Since strophe five does not identify its speaker, I cannot prove that the voice belongs to Jeremiah. Actually, silence about the identity of the speaker focuses attention solely upon the speech—which is replete with female semantics.

32. On end-stress, see Rudolf Bultmann, *The History of the Synoptic Tra-*

dition (ET: New York: Harper & Row, 1963), p. 191: "There is also the law of *End-stress*, i.e., the most important thing is left to the end." Bultmann follows Axel Olrik, "Epic Laws of Folk Narrative," in *The Study of Folklore*, ed. Alan Dundas (Englewood Cliffs, NJ: Prentice-Hall, 1965), pp. 129–141.

33. Professor Anderson pointed out this inclusive function to me.

34. Cf. the use of a rhetorical question in strophe four, v. 20a.

35. Bright, *Jeremiah*, op. cit.

36. Although these rubrics may have been, in the words of Holladay, "added secondarily," they belong to the final form of the poem, and it is this form that I am interpreting rhetorically; see note 17, above.

37. Cf. Genesis 1:27; 5:2, Isaiah 65:17–18.

38. The Hebrew order of words shows this alternation clearly: "For creates (innovation) Yahweh (continuation) a new thing (innovation) in the land (continuation)."

39. In offering a rhetorical interpretation of this colon, I may be rushing in where angels fear to tread. (At any rate, I have altered my earlier understanding; cf. *Interpreter's Dictionary of the Bible*, Supplementary Volume, p. 368.) As scholars have long observed, the colon is difficult to understand, even though its words are easy to translate. Cf. the varieties of interpretations in recent translations: RSV, JB, NEB, NAB. In the AB, Bright notes that "the meaning is wholly obscure and it might have been wiser to leave the colon blank" (op. cit., p. 282). My effort is to discern sense for these words in terms of the organic unity of the poem itself—an approach I share with Professor Anderson, although our results differ.

40. The phrase to "move between mystery and meaning" I borrow from Professor Hazelton (see "Theology and Metaphor"; also "Theological Analogy and Metaphor," a paper privately circulated).

41. Cf. Psalms 55:10; 59:6; 14; Jonah 2:3, 5.

42. Another debt to Professor Anderson, though we interpret this wordplay differently.

43. For *tʿsôbēb* (surround) as a verb giving power to God, see Deuteronomy 32:10; Psalm 32:7, 10.

44. My purpose is not to discuss all meanings of *geber* but to focus upon those that are congenial to the male images within this poem.

45. E.g., 1 Samuel 14:52; 17:51. For discussions of this verse that develop the meaning of *geber* as warrior or he-man, see William L. Holladay, "Jer. xxxi 22B Reconsidered: 'The Woman Encompasses the Man,'" *Vetus Testamentum*, 16 (1966): 236–39; "Jeremiah and Women's Liberation," *Andover Newton Quarterly*, 12 (March 1972): 213–23; *Jeremiah: Spokesman Out of Time* (New York: The Pilgrim Press, 1974), pp. 116–17.

46. My debt to new criticism is apparent; see especially Rene Wellek and Austin Warren, *Theory of Literature* (New York: Harcourt, Brace & World, 1956); Northrop Frye, *Anatomy of Criticism* (Princeton: Princeton University Press, 1957).

47. This is a slightly revised version of an article which was published originally in *Phoenix: New Directions in the Study of Man*, vol. III, no. 2, Fall/Winter 1979, pp. 25–37. It is published here by permission of Phoenix Associates, 164 Hawthorne Avenue, Palo Alto, CA 94301.

48. Edith Hamilton, *Mythology: Timeless Tales of Gods and Heroes* (New York and Scarborough, Ontario, 1942), p. 24.

49. "Divine realm" is here used to designate the belief system of a culture concerning the supernatural or extranormal, i.e., its mythology or theology.

50. To some extent this statement is true of Kate Millet, *Sexual Politics* (New York: Doubleday, 1970). We must remember, however, that the purpose of this book was to awaken people to social injustice.

51. Peter Green, *A Concise History of Ancient Greece* (London: London, Thames & Hudson, 1973), pp. 36–37; and Sarah B. Pomeroy, *Goddesses, Whores, Wives and Slaves: Women in Classical Antiquity* (New York: Schocken Books, 1975), chap. 1.

52. See D. A. Hester, "Recent Developments in Mediterranean 'Substrate' Studies," *Minos*, n.s., 9 (1968): 219–35.

53. Green, *Concise History*, loc. cit.

54. Gerald Cadogan raises this possibility in *Palaces of Minoan Crete* (London: Barde & Jenkins, 1976), p. 9.

55. Green, *Concise History*, p. 34.

56. Some scholars have argued for a matriarchy during this period, but I consider this an unlikely possibility. See Pomeroy, *Goddesses*, chap. 1, for arguments pro and con.

57. Robert E. Wolverton, *An Outline of Classical Mythology*, (Totowa, NJ: Littlefield, Adams, 1971), pp. 6ff.; and Michael Grant, *Myths of the Greeks and Romans* (Cleveland: World, 1962).

Hesiod's *Theogony*, composed around 700 B.C., was the earliest extant attempt to synthesize the various myths and establish a genealogy of the gods. Olympian goddesses such as Demeter, Athena, and Aphrodite were probably once local fertility goddesses who were incorporated into the pantheon as the Greeks expanded.

In the *Theogony*, Gaia (Earth) emerged from chaos and generated Ouranos (Heaven), the Hills, and Pontus (the Deep). She married Ouranos, and they produced Cyclops (one-eyed giants), Hekatoncheires (Hundred-handed Ones), and the Titans, including Kronos (Saturn) and Rhea. Kronos overthrew Ouranos, married Rhea, and begat the Olympians, one of whom was Zeus. Zeus in turn overthrew Kronos after a long battle with the Titans. The younger gods elected him third and perpetual King of Heaven, and he married his sister Hera, an ancient goddess of Argos (Mycenae).

58. Paul Thieme, "The Indo-European Language," *Scientific American*, October 1958, pp. 63–74.

59. Paul Friedrich, "Proto Indo-European Kinship," *Ethnology*, 5 (1966): 1–36. In particular, affinal terms, with one exception, referred to the wife's in-laws only, indicating that the bride went to live with her husband's family. The sole kinship term with the wife as linking relative was °*syēw-ro-* "wife's brother" (or surrogate), who probably became her protector after the death of her father.

60. Compare Sanskrit *dyāws* "sky."

61. Calvert Watkins, "Indo-European and the Indo-Europeans," in *American Heritage Dictionary* (New York: Houghton Mifflin Co., 1969–71), p. 1501.

The reconstructed word for "horse" is °*ekwo-*, and it may be based on the ancient root °*kwon-*, meaning "dog," giving further evidence for the late arrival of horses into the Indo-European community. (Expressions for "horse" are derived from "dog" in some American Indian languages.)

137

62. The Aztecs at first thought the horse and rider were a single animal.

63. Green, *Concise History*, p. 38.

64. Ibid., p. 30. See also Chester G. Starr, *The Ancient Greeks* (New York: Oxford University Press, 1971), chap. 4.

65. Cadogan, *Palaces*, loc. cit.

66. Ibid. p. 46.

67. J. T. Hooker, *Mycenean Greece* (London: Routledge & Kegan Paul, 1976), pp. 205–6.

68. Robert Graves, *The White Goddess: A Historical Grammar of Poetic Myth* (New York: Random House, 1948), pp. 51ff.

69. In the Homeric version, the dragon is a female oppressor of the people. Apollo slays her and builds the Delphic shrine and oracle. In other versions, the dragon is male and Apollo gains control of an established shrine from a goddess. See Joseph Fontenrose, *Python: A Study of Delphic Myth and Its Origins* (Berkeley and Los Angeles: University of California, 1959), Introduction.

70. The Medusa legend would indicate that masked priestesses were involved in the rites.

71. I. M. Lewis, *Ecstatic Religions* (Baltimore: Penguin Books, 1971), gives a full discussion of this phenomenon. In ancient times, the witches of Thessaly might have been such marginal people. Women held high positions in the Eleusinian mystery cult, which continued to worship the goddess Persephone, and they were the sole participants in the Thesmophoria, the agrarian festival in honor of Demeter (Pomeroy, *Goddesses*, pp. 75–78). Current examples are the many spiritualist groups and storefront churches whose leaders and members tend to be women or low-status men.

72. Nine poetesses of the Archaic Age (800 B.C. to 500 B.C.) were considered among the finest of the period, the greatest being Sappho of Lesbos (sixth century B.C.). Aristocratic women often received an advanced education in some Greek states, but the social leveling of Athenian democracy tended to remove even that possibility. Athens did not produce a single female poet (Pomeroy, *Goddesses*, p. 56).

73. Plato, *Republic*, ed. and trans. R. G. Bury (London, 1952), 454D–456C.

74. Aristotle, *"Poetics,"* in *Introduction to Aristotle*, ed. Richard McKeon (Chicago: University of Chicago Press, 1947), chap. 15.

75. Vern L. Bullock, *The Subordinate Sex: A History of Attitudes toward Women* (Chicago: University of Illinois, 1973), chap. 3. Paradoxically, female citizens had more rights in militaristic Sparta, where they moved about freely, had athletic contests, and participated in business matters, probably because they were forced to manage things while the men were away at war. Slave women, of course, had very little freedom anywhere.

76. If male envy were responsible for the decline of women in Greece, one would expect Homeric legends to be more misogynist than later Greek writings, but the reverse is the case. A woman's power becomes especially threatening to male status and self-esteem after women have been clearly defined as an inferior caste.

77. I do not deny the possibility of an unchanging ontological aspect to the divine, but attempts to clarify that aspect usually bring it into the dependent changeable realm under discussion.

78. When I propose this explanation, people sometimes ask me how the

Greeks could have let such developments take place. They forget that even more striking discrimination has occurred in our culture within the last century in favor of those able to get a college degree. Cultural survival now depends more on the technocrat than on the soldier, but degree requirements have spread to include the better jobs in most other areas. It is hard even to become an athlete in some sports without being admitted to a good university.

We should note that opportunities for well-born Greek women increased during the Hellenistic Age (323 B.C. to 30 B.C.), particularly outside of Athens. They were also high in Egypt and late Republican Rome. Many factors were involved, including the rise of an aristocracy and the end of small, warring independent states.

79. Samuel Noah Kramer, *The Sumerians: Their History, Culture, and Character* (Chicago: University of Chicago, 1963), chap. 2.

80. Ibid. p. 78.

81. Bullock, *Subordinate Sex*, p. 19.

82. As in Greek mythology, the goddesses were displaced by a third-generation god (Enlil). See Samuel Noah Kramer, *Sumerian Mythology: A Study of Spiritual and Literary Achievements in the Third Millennium B.C.* (Philadelphia: University of Pennsylvania, 1972), pp. 40–41.

83. James B. Pritchard, *The Ancient Near East: An Anthology of Texts and Pictures* (Princeton: Princeton University Press, 1958), pp. 31–39. Tiamat's only crime was to join a plot against the younger gods who had slain her husband. (She had previously pleaded with her husband to spare their lives.) Yet Tiamat rather than the bloody Marduk is automatically equated with the forces of chaos and darkness, even by modern scholars, which is the penalty of being the loser.

84. Bullock, *Subordinate Sex*, pp. 21ff.

85. Jehovah's "name" was YHVH, translated as "I Am That I Am." It was probably some form of the verb "to be" in Hebrew (usually rendered as "Yaweh"). It appears to be verbal rather than nominal. If so, it is not proper to speak of Jehovah as an entity at all, but rather as "being" or "becoming."

86. Lisa Lopez, "The Sexuality of God—Is He really a He?" Unpublished.

87. One possible exception was the levirate (later abolished), which was actually an extension of the general right of all people to have heirs.

88. Many Jews thought the Song of Songs represented the love of Yaweh for Israel, and Christians thought it expressed the love of God for the church. There is also a long tradition among mystics of describing union with God in terms of erotic love.

89. Ovid (*Metamorphoses*, Book 1) retells the creation story as if a god (*deus*) were the creator, although he concedes it might be nature (*nātūra*).

90. All biblical quotations are from the *King James Version*.

91. This passage, Ephesians 5:22–23, 28, proposes yet another analogical relationship: as man (generic) is to God, so let woman be to man (male), at least in the marriage relationship. It is rather shocking in view of the First Commandment, which restricts such reverence to God alone. I wonder that no feminist has ever accused Paul of advocating idolatry. It is only fair, however, to point out that biblical scholars are in disagreement over the intent of Paul's message.

92. See Millet, *Sexual Politics*, pp. 36–37.

93. Bullock, *Subordinate Sex*, pp. 160–70.

94. Heinrich Kramer and James Sprenger, The *Malleus Maleficarum*, trans. Montague Sommers (New York: Dover, 1971; published in 1928). The first sentence is a quote from Ecclesiasticus.

95. Ibid.

96. Marina Warner, *Alone of All Her Sex: The Myth and the Cult of the Virgin Mary* (New York: Knopf, 1976).

97. Dagmar Lorenz, "Nachwort," in Martin Luther, *Vom ehelichen Leben* (Stuttgart: Reclam, 1978).

98. Paradoxically, this asceticism is largely of late pagan origin, especially from the Neo-Platonists, Orphics, and Neo-Pythagoreans (Bullock, *Subordinate Sex*, chap. 5).

99. I am not including "coming-of-age" stories or the *Bildungsroman*. These genres usually describe initiation experiences into a contemporary value system rather than a conscious search for universal values.

100. The majority of the Indo-European forms and etymologies were taken from Carl Darling Buck, *A Dictionary of Selected Synonyms in the Principal Indo-European Languages* (Chicago: University of Chicago, 1949), pp. 79–85. There is disagreement over the exact form of some of the reconstructions, particularly °$\widehat{gh}_bm\bar{o}n$ "human" (not taken from Buck).

101. We must remember, however, that reconstruction cannot recover all the forms nor does it necessarily represent a uniform time period.

102. Sometimes a word meaning "man male" shifted again to mean "husband" with a new coinage for "man male" (i.e., Russian *muž* "husband," *mužčina* "man male").

103. Likewise, Hebrew *adām* "person, earthling" was used to designate a male. Of course, there are many cases where the expected meaning shift did not take place, such as Celtic.

104. See Buck, *Dictionary,* loc. cit.

105. Nils M. Holmer, "The Character of the Iroquoian Languages," *Uppsala Canadian Studies,* 1 (1952): 22–23. Holmer comments that high-ranking Iroquoian women were, in effect, "the people" (that is, "the people who counted"). Likewise, in strongly patriarchal cultures, landowners and arms-bearing men would be "the people who counted."

Wallace L. Chafe lists Seneca *ᶻoᐧkweh* only in the meaning "person," apparently contradicting Holmer, although different usages could be involved (*Seneca Morphology and Dictionary,* [Washington, D.C.: Smithsonian Press, 1967]). Various prefixes meaning "she," however, also function as sex-indefinite markers.

106. Again we have the paradox that the Iroquois were warlike. But the territorial expansion practiced by the Indo-Europeans was rare in North America before the white man came, so cultural survival was more dependent upon agriculture than the warrior.

107. I owe this formulation to Georgia Whippo Fuller.

108. The doctrine that language largely determines worldview is known as the Whorf Hypothesis, although it had a long history before Benjamin Lee Whorf.

109. We have only to look at the history of forced changes in language to realize the truth of this statement. Slow learners were once called "dumb" or "dull." To avoid such stigma, educators insisted on referring to them as

"retarded," which soon acquired all the connotations of "dumb." New locutions were subsequently employed, the most recent of which is "special." Likewise, the poor were renamed "underpriviledged," which did not raise their salaries a bit. After that term became taboo, they were called "disadvantaged." Change in language without prior change in the social order simply leads to a chain of euphemistic substitutions.

110. The Orthodox view is similar except that the Father generates the Holy Spirit through the Son instead of jointly with the Son.

111. To make matters more complex, Christ was supposedly conceived by the Holy Spirit.

112. See note 78. Like skill in arms, the mental ability necessary to run a technological society need not be associated with creativity or compassion. Both technocrats and the military tend to support the status quo.

113. Margaret Wood, "The Potential for Success or Failure of Suggested Replacements," 1975, unpublished. "Chairperson of the committee" and "Ms. Adams" were embedded in a questionnaire with sixteen other items including "worker," "professor," "sinner." Subjects were asked to give first impressions including age, sex (male, female, either), probable life-style, marital status.

114. Margaret Mitschu, "The Potential for Success or Failure of Suggested Replacements: A Follow Up Survey," 1975, unpublished.

115. Kathie Miller, "Sexism in Language," 1977, unpublished.

116. Lori Ward, "The Attempt at Euphemistic Substitutions—Has It Been Successful?" 1977, unpublished.

117. The Pope's decision underscores the power of the concrete analogy. "When Christ's role in the Eucharist is to be expressed sacramentally, there would not be this natural resemblance which must exist between Christ and his minister if the role of Christ were not taken by a man."

The "resemblance" in question is physical, which the Catholic Church supposedly places below the spiritual. It ignores the fact that the Christian virtues of faith, piety, and submission to the law of God are more frequently practiced by women than by men.

118. Certain Catholic theologians are thinking along these lines. See Mary Daly, "After the Death of God the Father," *Commonweal*, March 12, 1971, pp. 7–11.

119. "Reflection" by Phyllis Kuestner. Used by permission.

Selected
Bibliography

Resources (Poems, Songbooks, Liturgies)

Because We Are One People. Ecumenical Women's Center, 1653 West School Street, Chicago, IL, 60657, 1974. A compilation of revised standard hymns.

Brock, Fred, ed. *Hymns for the Family of God.* Alexandria, IN: Alexandria House, 1976.

Courtot, Martha. *Journey.* San Francisco: Pearlchild, 1977.

———. *Tribe.* San Francisco: Pearlchild, 1977.

Crotwell, Helen Gray, ed. *Women and the Word.* Philadelphia: Fortress Press, 1978. A collection of sermons.

"Expanding Our Language About God," Church Leadership Resources, Box 179, St. Louis, MO, 63166.

"Expanding Our Language About Humanity," Church Leadership Resources, Box 179, St. Louis, MO 63166.

Gill, Elaine, ed. *Mountain Moving Day: An Anthology of Women's Poetry.* Trumansburg, NY: Crossing Press, 1973.

Grana, Janice, ed. *Images: Women in Transition.* Winona, MN: St. Mary's College Press, 1977.

Haugerud, Joann. *The Word for Us.* Coalition on Women and Religion, 4759 15th Avenue NE, Seattle, WA 98105. The Gospels restated in inclusive language.

Neufer Emsweiler, Sharon and Tom. *Sisters and Brothers Sing.* Wesley Foundation Campus Ministry, 211 North School Street, Normal, IL. A songbook with worship resources in the back.

———. *Women and Worship.* New York: Harper & Row, 1974. Nonsexist liturgies.

Parker, Alice. *Creative Hymn Singing.* Chapel Hill, NC: Hinshaw Music, 1976.

Ritual in a New Day: An Invitation. Nashville: Abingdon Press, 1976.

Silverman, Jerry. *Liberated Woman's Songbook,* ed. Robert Markel. New York: Macmillan Co., 1971.

Sing a Womansong. Ecumenical Women's Center, 1653 West School Street, Chicago, IL 60657.

Stahl, Carolyn. *Opening to God: Guided Imagery and Meditation on Scripture*. Nashville: The Upper Room, 1977.

Swidler, Arlene, ed. *Sistercelebrations*. Philadelphia: Fortress Press, 1974.

Withers, Barbara, ed. *Language About God in Liturgy and Scripture*. Published for Joint Educational Development by the Geneva Press, 1979. Available from The Program Agency, Church Education Services, 475 Riverside Drive, New York, NY, 10027.

Woman-soul Flowing: Words for Personal and Communal Reflection. Ecumenical Women's Center, 1653 West School Street, Chicago, IL.

Worship: Inclusive Language Resources. Church Leadership Resources, Box 179, St. Louis, MO 63166, 1977, No. CL36772M.

Articles, Books, Commentaries

Althouse, LaVonne, and Snook, Lois, eds. *In God's Image: Toward Wholeness for Women and Men*. New York: Division for Mission in North America, Lutheran Church in America, 1976.

Bosmajian, Haig. *Language of Oppression*. Washington, DC: Public Affairs Press, 1974.

Clark, Elizabeth, and Richardson, Herbert. *Woman and Religion: A Feminist Sourcebook of Christian Thought*. New York: Harper & Row, 1977.

Clark, Linda. "We Are Also Sarah's Children." *Drew Gateway*, Spring 1978 (Women in Ministry issue).

Goldstein, Valerie Saiving. "The Human Situation: A Feminine View." *Journal of Religion*, vol. 40 (1960).

Key, Mary Ritchie. *Male/Female Language*. Metuchen, NJ: Scarecrow Press, 1975.

Lakoff, Robin. *Language and Women's Place*. New York: Harper & Row, 1975.

"Language About God 'Opening the Door.'" Published by the Task Force on Language About God, Advisory Council on Discipleship and Worship, United Presbyterian Church in the U.S.A., 475 Riverside Drive, New York, NY 10027, 1975.

Listening: Journal of Religion and Culture. Issue entitled "Women and Religion," vol. 13 (Spring 1978).

Miller, Casey, and Swift, Kate. *Words and Women: New Language in New Times*. Garden City, N.Y.: Doubleday, 1976.

Mollenkott, Virginia. *Women, Men and the Bible*. Nashville: Abingdon Press, 1977.

Morton, Nelle, "The Rising Woman Consciousness in a Male Language Structure." Available from the Ecumenical Women's Center, 1653 West School Street, Chicago, IL 60657.

Pomeroy, Sarah B. *Goddesses, Whores, Wives, and Slaves: Women in Classical Antiquity*. New York: Schocken Books, 1975.

"The Power of Language Among the People of God." Task Force on Language About God, Advisory Council on Discipleship and Worship, United Presbyterian Church in the U.S.A., 475 Riverside Drive, New York, NY 10027.

Rosaldo, Michelle Zimbalist, and Lamphere, Louise. *Women, Culture, and Society*. Stanford: Stanford University Press, 1973.

Russell, Letty, ed. *The Liberating Word: A Guide to Non-Sexist Interpretation of the Bible*. Philadelphia: Westminster Press, 1976.

Samuels, Mike and Nancy. *Seeing with the Mind's Eye*. New York: Random House, 1975.

Trible, Phyllis. *God and the Rhetoric of Sexuality*. Philadelphia: Fortress Press, 1978.

White, James F. *New Forms of Worship*. Nashville: Abingdon Press, 1971.